Guardians

The Secret Life of Goalies

GARY MASON & BARBARA GUNN

Andrews McMeel
Publishing

Kansas City

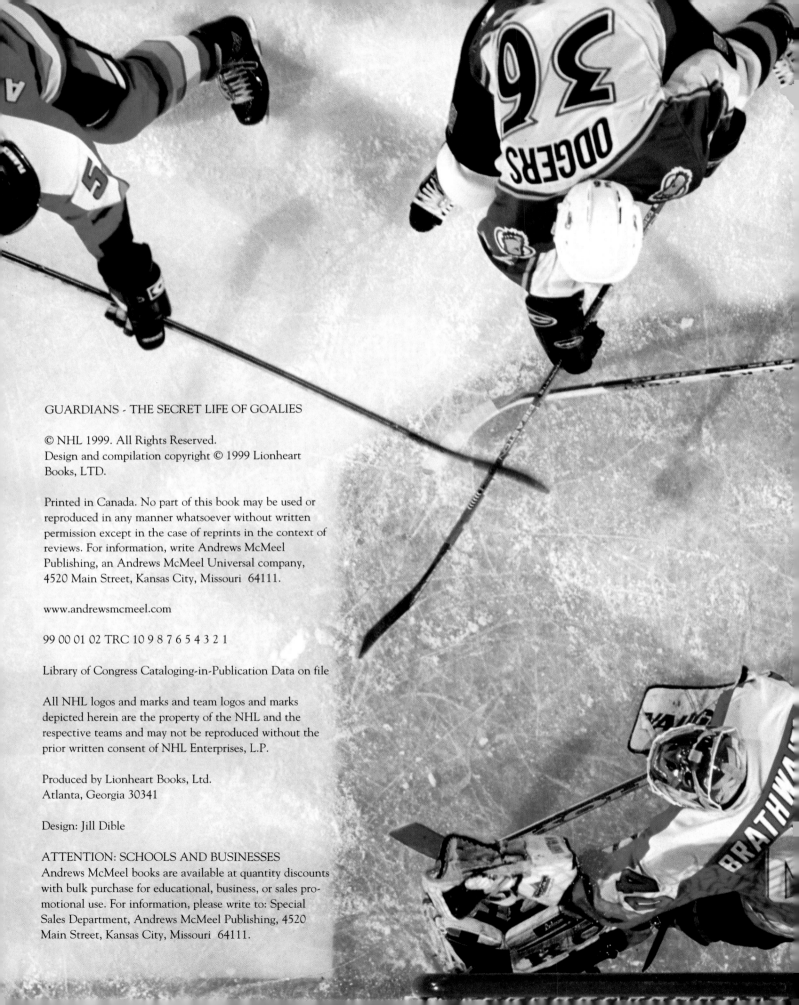

Table of Contents

Introduction

"Goalies are different," the great Montreal Canadiens netminder Ken Dryden once reflected.

"Whether it's because the position attracts certain personality types or only permits certain ones to succeed; whether the experience is so intense and fundamental that it transforms its practitioners to type—I don't know the answer. But whatever it is, the differences between 'players' and 'goalies' are manifest and real."

Who are these masked men? And what strange forces draw them to one of the most demanding positions in all of sport?

As hockey prepares to enter the 21st century, never has the position of goaltender been under a brighter spotlight. Never have so many of the NHL's greatest stars been the players who stop the pucks, not just the ones who shoot them.

The 1990s may be remembered as a golden age for the position. For the first time, a goaltender was named the NHL's most valuable player not just one year, but twice in a row. And the Buffalo Sabres Dominik Hasek, who also won his fifth Vezina trophy this past season, is only one of the backstoppers who have taken the position and standard of play to soaring new heights.

And yet, despite all the attention goaltenders have received in recent years, they remain a puzzling group of individuals—unique athletes who form an almost secret society. And unless you have played the position, at the highest levels, under unbearable pressure, unless you have been part of this exclusive club, you can't begin to understand all the attendant skill, steely nerve and uncommon composure it takes to become a member.

While teams insist on unity and togetherness, a goalie is the one player a team allows to be different. He can sit by himself, if he wishes, and slip inside a cone of silence before a game. As he prepares to lead his team into battle, a goalie knows he's the last line of defense, often the final person standing between victory and defeat.

The position has attracted its share of eccentrics, and their stories lay the foundation for the widespread reputation goalies carry as wackos and oddballs. No one can forget the stories about former Philadelphia Flyers goaltender Bob Froese, who wouldn't change his underwear when he was on a winning streak. And then there was Gilles Gratton, who played for the St. Louis Blues and the New York Rangers and had the strange habit of skating around the ice before and after practice wearing nothing but a jockstrap.

Today, Toronto Maple Leafs goalie Curtis Joseph would no more think of streaking around the ice after a morning workout, than he would contemplate entering a game without his mask.

Yes, the mask. If there is one piece of equipment that, more than anything, revolutionized the position of goaltender it is the face mask. Now, goalies like Joseph and Hasek, rising stars like Boston's Byron Dafoe and San Jose's Steve Shields, just shake their heads at the thought of what their predecessors did.

Today's masks are so well constructed, goalies like Dominik Hasek have even taken to intentionally stopping pucks with their heads. Progressive developments with just about every other piece of equipment a goaltender wears have made the position, in many people's opinion, the safest in hockey.

And this has had two sweeping ramifications.

First, today's guardians of the net are fearless. Slapshots travelling 100 mph, while still not the friendliest of sights, don't unnerve goalies the way they once did. This has made goalies bolder, more confident and generally improved their performance.

Second, because the position isn't as high risk as it once was, it is attracting more and better athletes. Once upon a time, perhaps the brave men who guarded the net without any face protection were a little wacky. Stories about the 400 stitches that former Detroit goaltender Terry Sawchuk took on his head during his career likely deterred many fine athletes from checking out the position.

Not anymore.

Goaltending in the NHL has never been better. Maybe even a little too good, in fact—in the last couple of years the league has looked for ways to eliminate some of the perceived advantages the modern-day equipment has given netminders. Today there are recently introduced rules governing everything from the size of a goalie's glove to the width of his pads.

Yes, there's no question that the goaltender has become one of the coolest positions in all of sport. Nevertheless, while today's NHL goaltender basks in the newfound attention and affection, he still inhabits a lonely world.

"Playing goal is not fun," Ken Dryden once said, referring to the enormous weight a goalie bears.

Like baseball's pitcher and football's quarterback, hockey's goaltender goes into every game knowing any mistake he makes will be seen by thousands. The red light blinking behind him drawing even more attention to his every error. One minute he can be his team's hero, enjoying chants from the crowd. The next he can be the goat, gazing out at the disappointed faces on his teammates, listening to chants that have become rants.

It is a pressure that even the game's greatest stars fret about. A pressure that will always define the position and the person playing it.

"I get nervous before every game," says Dominik Hasek, the man considered by many to be the greatest goalie in the world. "Every game I know I have to stop the puck. If I do we win, and if I don't we lose."

It's that simple.

Rituals

We all know what the thinking is. Goaltenders are wackos, misfits, eccentric screwballs. After all, we're told, no one with half a brain would consider strapping a pair of pillows to his shins and willingly stand there, waiting to be assailed by flying rubber.

We're all aware of the stereotype. Goalies are unhinged. Goalies are nut cases. Goalies are lunatics who are so stressed-out by the job at hand that they do peculiar things like skate in circles before the opening face-off, or whack the posts for good luck, or recite some secret mantra.

More than anything, the guardian of the net has long been reputed to be the most superstitious guy on the planet, an oddball who'd sooner live without a mirror than take a chance on breaking one.

But stereotypes are, well, stereotypes, and truth is something else. Fact is, the men who guard the hockey nets are anything but crazy. Courageous, yes. Eccentric, sometimes. But no, never crazy.

After all, you may be a tad peculiar to want to stand in front of a goalie net, but you have to be mighty sharp to stay there.

That's not to say, however, that the position hasn't had a cast of colorful characters. And yes, it's also true that many of them have developed their personal pre-game rituals, quirky little rites designed to get the gray matter focused, to elicit a bit of luck, or to simply scare away the jitters.

Whether these rites work remains to be seen, but one thing about them is certain: they rep-

resent something about this particular breed of men that only goalies can comprehend. For if goaltending is anything, it's a kind of secret society, a clandestine fraternity whose members are the only ones who really understand each other.

These days, it's probably fair to say that there are fewer big-time goalies who adhere to some kind of pre-game ritual than in days gone by. Neither Philadelphia's John Vanbiesbrouck nor Boston's Byron Dafoe, for example, consider themselves remotely superstitious.

Still, there's no shortage of other contemporary netminders who follow intricate rituals prior to a game, Patrick Roy being one of them. But as a gander through hockey's history books reveals, Roy doesn't hold a lock on goalie superstitions.

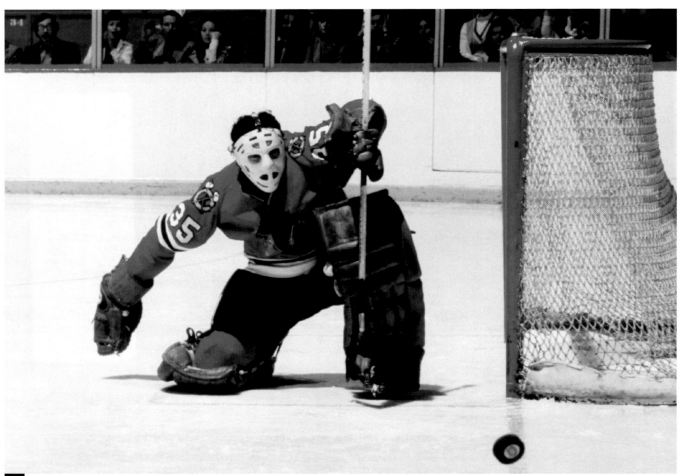

Tony Esposito's habit, reportedly shared by the great Russian goalie Vladislav Tretiak, was to be quiet—completely quiet. The three-time Vezina trophy winner wouldn't speak to anyone on the day of a game, not even to his wife and children when they were driving to the arena. When Esposito was on a road trip, the same thing applied: he wouldn't speak on game days.

Lorne Chabot, a Vezina-winner who played with the New York Rangers as well as Toronto, Montreal and Chicago, had a pre-game routine that was probably more practical than superstitious: he shaved. And in the days preceding goalie masks, that made a heck of a lot of sense. "I stitch better when my skin is smooth," he would explain.

Sean Burke, who's tended the net for New Jersey, Hartford and Vancouver and is currently standing between the pipes in Florida, also has a pre-game plan that seems fairly innocuous. He eats his meals at the same time, he drives to the rink the same way, and he changes his skate laces, whether they need to be changed or not.

Bernie Wolfe, who tended goal for the Washington Capitals in the 1970s, recalls fellow netminder Gary Inness, who not only got dressed before a game, and took shots before a game, but also lined up Dixie cups before a game.

"Gary had to have ice on the right side of the cups and water on the left and a wet towel on the right side and a dry towel on the left," Wolfe once told broadcaster Dick Irvin when he was researching a book on goaltending. "God forbid one of the kids working in the dressing room would mix everything up. He would go completely nuts."

But it was Inness's other pre-game ritual, the more, well, demonstrative one, that people tended to notice, and that may have helped to perpetuate the stereotype of the unbalanced goalie.

"Gary used to throw up before a game if he knew he was playing," says Wolfe.

"One night I got the start and got bombed early so they yanked me. When I was skating to the bench we were passing each other and I apologized to him for not giving him a chance to be sick. But he got sick anyway. He played the rest of the period, went into the dressing room, and got sick."

He wouldn't have been the first. Glenn Hall, a member of the Hockey Hall of Fame who was tending nets two decades before Inness saw any action, had the same habit. He, too, would convulse and vomit before many a game.

The great Patrick Roy may not put a lot of stock in throwing up prior to a game, but he certainly has his other little rituals. He writes the names of his

> For if goaltending is anything, it's a kind of secret society, a clandestine fraternity whose members are the only ones who really understand each other.

3

"When Roy hits the ice, he takes his superstitions with him. He refuses to skate on the red or blue lines. He talks— yes, talks—to the goal posts.

kids on his stick before battle. He dons his equipment in the same order. He plays with a puck in the dressing room, first bouncing it on the floor, then laying it on the ground, always to his right.

He doesn't leave the rituals in the dressing room. When Roy hits the ice, he takes his superstitions with him. He refuses to skate on the red or blue lines. He skates in circles in the corners after a whistle. And before every game he skates out of the net, turns around and talks—yes, talks—to the goalposts.

Ed Belfour of the Dallas Stars is another contemporary goalie who has some rigorous habits that he adheres to prior to every game. The Vezina winner is meticulous—some would say

obsessed—about his pre-game exercise routine, and is so preoccupied with ensuring his equipment is in top condition that he's been known to spend up to six hours at the skate sharpener trying to get the perfect edge for his skates.

It's impossible, of course, to know whether any of this has any effect on the way Roy or Belfour play their game, but that's probably beside the point. If Roy believes he can drive away his pre-game demons by bouncing a hockey puck, then that's really all that matters.

In the case of Bob Froese, it was the underwear that mattered. Froese, who played first with Philadelphia and later with the New York Rangers, had one particular quirk that he adhered to, not simply prior to the game, but throughout the game—and beyond.

"I had a few superstitions," admits Froese, "and one of them was that I didn't change my underwear if I was on a winning streak."

During one stretch, Froese went 11 games unbeaten, and the washer never ran. "There was one reason my wife was glad I retired," he says.

At least he wore underwear. That was something you couldn't always say about Gilles Gratton. Gratton, a quirky netminder for both St. Louis and the New York Rangers who believed in reincarnation and was said to believe that his fate as a goaltender was punishment for stoning people during biblical times, is reputed to have sometimes walked around the ice before and after practice—in nothing but a jockstrap.

Goaltending has had its cast of characters, no question about that. Even the legendary Jacques Plante has gone down in history, not only for being a seven-time Vezina winner and the first goalie to regularly wear a mask, but also as the guy who liked to blow kisses to the crowd and knit toques, which he occasionally wore during games.

Sure, goaltending has had its characters, and even its occasional oddballs. And when you take a look at some of them, you can understand how the stereotype developed.

"The stereotype comes from when the guys didn't wear masks," suggests Philadelphia's Vanbiesbrouck, one goalie who has no supersti-

Most games appeared in
by a goaltender, career:
Terry Sawchuk - 971

Most consecutive complete games
by a goaltender:
Glenn Hall - 502

Most games appeared in
by a goaltender, one season:
Grant Fuhr -79

Most minutes played
by a goaltender, one season:
Martin Brodeur - 4,433

Most minutes played
by a goaltender, career:
Terry Sawchuk - 57,228

Most shutouts, career:
Terry Sawchuk - 103

Most shutouts, one season:
George Hainsworth - 22

tions. "I mean, guys throwing up and not wearing masks—a combination that sends a certain message."

Vanbiesbrouck's observation is probably right on: even though the NHL's contemporary goaltenders face incredible pressure as they crouch before their posts, the fear factor is probably considerably less than what it used to be. After all, when you're someone like a Glenn Hall, and you're standing there without a mask for most of your career waiting for a shooter like Rocket Richard to fire the rubber bullet directly at your face, you can be excused for developing a few quirky habits.

"I hate every minute I play," Hall once said. "I'm sick to my stomach before the game, between periods, and from the start of the season to the end. I sometimes ask myself, 'What the hell am I doing out here?' "

But today, says Philadelphia's Vanbiesbrouck,

> "I hate every minute I play. I'm sick to my stomach before the game, between periods, and from the start of of the season to the end. I sometimes ask myself, 'What the hell am I doing out here?' "

developments in goalie equipment have done much to eliminate the dangers faced by hockey's guardians.

"Everybody thinks we're crazy," he says, "but I'm telling you, it's the safest position out there."

Safer, certainly. But even though there are fewer members of this unique association who are prone to throwing up prior to a hockey game, and none who'd likely rip around a rink semi-naked, hockey's netminders face the same unrelenting pressure they've always faced. They still have a job that differs from their teammates, and a role, say many of them, that no one else can truly comprehend.

"Nobody understands the position who hasn't played it," John Garrett, goaltender for Hartford, Quebec and Vancouver, once said. "Hockey is a team game, but for a goalie, it's more like an individual sport."

Chico Resch would be in complete agreement. Resch, who tended the NHL nets for the New York Islanders, Colorado, New Jersey and Philadelphia, has observed that a goaltender is a unique player on a hockey team.

"Goalies are different, no question about it. It takes a special kind of guy to go through what a goalie goes through, practice after practice, game after game."

They're special, all right, special because, in this fraternity, there's a kind of on-ice stress that's not nearly as intense if you happen to be a winger, say, or a defenseman.

"There are unique pressures on goaltenders,"

says Joel Fish, director of the Center for Sports Psychology. "It boils down to this: nobody can cover for them. A forward or a defenseman can make a mistake and get away with it, because somebody can cover for them. A goalie doesn't have that luxury."

Little wonder, then, that some of them do funny things like change their laces before a game. Little wonder that they might eat at the same time, or be so preoccupied with the coming game that they don't want to talk to anybody.

Little wonder that theirs is a unique world, a secret society that's accessible only to those who wear the pads.

Gary Smith tended nets for so many National Hockey League teams—eight in 14 years—he earned the nickname "Suitcase." He knows, like everyone else who's ever guarded a hockey net, that the crease is a

lonely place, and that only a goaltender can truly appreciate that.

"Now, with goalie coaches, there's someone else to talk to," says Smith. "But at one time, other than the other goalie, there was really no one."

Goalies had only each other, and in many ways, they still do. After all, only a goaltender can really know what it's like to stand before the posts, waiting for a slapshot.

True, they've always been considered a little bit different. But when you think about it, when you really think about the kind of courage it must take to do what they do, game after game after game, you start to believe that, yes, they really are a different breed entirely.

Dominik Hasek

39   BUFFALO SABRES

Before he became Superman, before the Vezinas and league MVPs. Before an Olympic gold medal was placed around his neck and he was handed the title, World's Greatest Goalie, there was a time when Dominik Hasek wondered if he had what it takes to make it in the National Hockey League.

It was in the early 1990s, and Hasek was stuck in Indianapolis, minding the nets for a farm team of the Chicago Blackhawks. Hasek had been called up to the big team a few times, but it never seemed to matter how well he played. Eddie Belfour was the main guy in the Windy City in those days and Dominik Hasek was nothing more than a minor league insurance policy.

If you have to hit rock bottom before you get to climb life's highest mountains, Hasek had found Death Valley. For the first time in his career, Hasek skated out to his net to start games not caring about the outcome. "There was one incredible game where they scored on me nine times," Hasek would remember about his days in Indianapolis. "I had never been through anything like that before. It was so bad I almost liked it."

Hasek? Nine goals? The thought is almost inconceivable now.

The reserves of confidence that Hasek had built up during a brilliant amateur and professional career in

his homeland of the Czech Republic, were nearly depleted.

"A goalie's mistake can cost you all the hard work of 20 players," Hasek said. "That's scary, so you need a lot of confidence. You need to have the trust of the coach, the other players, the fans ... I didn't have it. So you start doubting yourself: Am I still good enough? Do I still have it?" As we know now, Hasek still had it. In fact, he was yet to explore the full bounds of his greatness. A trade from Chicago to Buffalo in 1992 would be the key that would unlock the treasure chest of awards and accolades that would be his the rest of the decade.

What can you say about Dominik Hasek?

One day, years from now, people will still shake their heads over many of his accomplishments. They will marvel that one man, under pressure few athletes in any sport face, managed to perform so masterfully, so consistently.

But his shutouts or goals against averages won't be Hasek's greatest legacy to the game of hockey. No, above all else—and this is the mark of true greatness—the skinny kid from Pardubice will be remembered for how he changed the position he played. Hasek's unorthodox style—his flailing arms and legs, his habit of dropping his stick to pick up the puck with his blocker hand, his penchant for stopping pucks with his head—would breed a new generation of imitators.

"People go to watch Hasek because he's an entertainer; he lifts them out of their seats," says former Boston Bruins goalie, Gerry Cheevers.

"He uses his glove, his blocker, his stick, his legs, his chest like other goalies. But he's so different because he also uses his back and stomach when he scrambles around like a snow angel on the ice. Hell, I'd swear I've also seen him use his head—on purpose—to stop a shot."

In 1997, Hasek, became the first goalie since Jacques Plante in 1962 to be named league MVP. He would win the award the following year too. His bid for a third straight MVP award this past season wasn't to be, however, as fellow Czech countryman Jaromir Jagr of the Pittsburgh Penguins, would end Hasek's streak.

However, Hasek would add another Vezina trophy to his shelf—his fifth, following another spectacular season between the pipes. Hasek's goals against average was an incredible 1.87, evidence of the kind of play that helped take his team to the Stanley Cup finals.

Again, Hasek was often brilliant in his battle with Dallas Stars netminder, Eddie Belfour, during the cup finals. But it was Belfour, Hasek's former teammate with the Blackhawks, who would seize the day and lead the Stars to their first-ever Cup victory. Hasek would have to wait another year to try and lay claim to one of the few trophies he hasn't put his hands around.

Meanwhile, *Goalies World*, the magazine bible of goaltending, would name Hasek the world's top goaltender for the fifth time. The magazine compared what Hasek has done for goaltending to what Wayne Gretzky accomplished in his career:

"Gretzky is the only player who ever had 200 - point seasons ... Hasek is the only goaltender who ever had a 93 percent save percentage after a complete season. Hasek just finished a fifth season with a 93 percent save percentage or better. Five times he has done what nobody else has ever done. That's how dominant he is."

There was never any doubt which position Dominik Hasek would play.

"Ever since I can remember, I always made straight for the goal," Hasek recalls. "In hockey, soccer, everything."

Hasek's father was a miner who only came home on weekends. But his father was home the day they held hockey tryouts for six-year-olds. The family couldn't afford good skates for Dominik. Instead, he had blades that screwed to the bottom of his shoes.

A group of nine-year-olds also staging tryouts at the time didn't have a goalie. Tall for his age, Hasek stuck up his hand and got the job. He'd never play hockey with kids his own age again until he became a professional.

Young Dominik became a student of the game early. He'd go to watch the practices of older kids. He studied the goalies. He made mental notes of how they were scored upon. And he came up with his own ideas about stopping the puck that he'd try out at his own practices.

But it was Hasek's remarkable flexibility that caught many people's attention. Double-jointed, he could do a kneeling split.

"The doctors always used to shake their heads when I did it," Hasek said. But beyond being able to see plays develop like none of his peers, and beyond his amazing elasticity, perhaps the greatest weapon Hasek had was his hatred of being scored upon.

"Dominik was always furious when he got scored on," said Otakar Mares, a Czech hockey veteran who coached Hasek for six years as a boy. "But he was only furious with himself. He never took his anger out on the other kids."

As a youngster, Hasek particularly loved working on stopping breakaways. After regular practice was over, Hasek would plead with teammates to stay on the ice and see if they could score on him in 10 breakaway chances. If they did, he would challenge them again. And again.

> One day, years from now, people will still shake their heads over many of Hasek's accomplishments. They will marvel that one man, under pressure few athletes in any sport face, managed to perform so masterfully, so consistently.

The practice paid off. Hasek would eventually establish a reputation as the hardest goalie in the world to score upon on a breakaway.

Hasek worked just as hard off the ice, too.

He earned the equivalent of a masters degree in history. And he was just as competitive when it came to his marks.

"I had to be No. 1 on my exams," Hasek said once. "I had to know everything. I had to be perfect or I'd rather not say anything. In hockey, I want to be perfect in net or I don't play."

Before coming to North America, Hasek had established himself as the top goalie in the Czech leagues. It was while playing for his hometown of Pardubice, that Hasek was drafted by the Blackhawks in the 11th round. Hasek wouldn't become aware of it until informed by an acquaintance a couple of months after the fact. While reluctant to leave friends and family, Hasek knew if he was going to pursue his dream to play in the NHL he would have to leave the homeland he loved and friends he was close to.

Few knew what to make of Hasek or his goaltending style when he first showed up at a Blackhawks training camp. It was so different from the stand-up or butterfly style that was so pervasive in the NHL. In fact, it was hard to characterize Hasek's style at all.

"He flops around the ice like a fish," Darryl Sutter, an assistant coach with the Blackhawks, said at the time. Chicago head coach Mike Keenan never was completely comfortable with Hasek's style. Truth be told, Keenan didn't need to spend a lot of time sizing up other goalies—he was quite happy with the No. 1 guy he had—Ed Belfour.

Hasek would see limited action with the Blackhawks, and he worried about his career. By 1992, Hasek's NHL dreams looked to be going nowhere. And he wasn't a kid anymore. He was nearly 28. Hockey's biological clock was ticking.

Ironically, it was while in a Blackhawks uniform that Hasek would first show the world his potential. It was during the final game of the Pittsburgh Penguins, four-game sweep over Chicago in the '92 Stanley Cup finals. Keenan pulled Belfour partway through the game and called Hasek's name.

Hasek was brilliant.

He stopped four Mario Lemieux breakaways and any number of point-blank shots from the Pittsburgh captain's teammates. He saved shots standing up, he saved them lying down. It didn't matter. It was one fabulous playoff performance.

When Hasek was traded to Buffalo that summer, he was put in the hands of former Sabres' goalie coach Mitch Korn. Korn will never forget what his memo to team management said after watching Hasek play for awhile.

"The guy can play . . . you just have to have a strong stomach to watch him." Korn helped refine Hasek's game.

"If Dom's game required anything it was patience," said Korn. "He knew what was going on and he reacted so fast, so early, it allowed the player a chance to react, and then Dom was all over the place."

"In general, once he developed that patience

he was rarely out of position. He rarely beats himself."

And before long, Hasek was inside the head of some of the game's greatest players.

"He's got an advantage on a lot of shooters because of the reputation he's built up as The Dominator," says Toronto Maple Leaf sharpshooter, Mats Sundin.

"I know I feel that way. When I come in alone on him, I think I have to try something special to score a goal. And that definitely gives him a psychological edge."

The Great One, Wayne Gretzky, who retired from hockey last season, said of Hasek: "He doesn't have a weakness, and you don't know what he's going to do."

Away from the rink, Hasek spends time with his wife, Alena, and two children and is often found immersed in a book about history or art. He also continues to find time for an old love —chess.

"He could be a chess grand master if he

wanted to," said Joseph Safar, a Buffalo surgeon and friend of Hasek's.

While the NHL has been the place where Hasek's legend has grown, it was the Nagano Olympics in 1998 where the goaltender would enjoy his greatest moment.

In a semi-final hockey game against Canada, Hasek put on one of the greatest goaltending performances of his life. The game was tied 1-1 after regulation and overtime and had to be settled by shootout.

Back in the Czech Republic his countrymen held their breath. His mother, Marie, couldn't stand to watch, so she wandered up and down the stairs of her apartment instead.

"All I heard were people screaming from the other apartments," said Marie. "Then my daughter came running up to me saying, 'We won, we won.'" Yes, they won. In the shootout, Canada's Patrick Roy wouldn't be quite as perfect as Hasek. While Roy let in one goal in the shootout, Hasek would stone Canada's Theo Fleury, Ray Bourque, Joe Nieuwendyk, Eric Lindros and Brendan Shanahan.

The Czechs would end up beating Russia in the gold medal final. About 70,000 fans watched the game on three huge screens in the town square back in Prague. And when the final horn sounded, the fireworks began and the champagne flowed in the city's streets.

Hasek and his teammates would return to Prague as conquering heroes. But there was only one person that the people wanted to see and wanted to hear—Hasek.

"Hasek to the Castle," they screamed, which means, roughly, Hasek for president. At her home, someone taped the words *Hasek Neni Clovek, Hasek Je Buh*, to the door of Marie Hasek's home. Translated, the words read:

Hasek is not a human being, Hasek is God.

When he returned to his home in Prague at the end of NHL season, Hasek would be mobbed every where he went. He decided to enforce a policy of not signing autographs for people who knocked on his door at home.

"One day a 60-year-old man came to my house," remembered Hasek. "I told him I don't give autographs and he started to cry. I felt so bad. He said: 'I don't feel bad because you won't give me an autograph. I feel happy because of what you did at the Olympics.'"

To commemorate one of the greatest moments in Czech history, the country made a stamp with Hasek's image on it.

The little kid from Pardubice had come a long way. A long way indeed.

As a kid growing up in the industrial town of Pardubice, Czechoslovakia, Dominik Hasek never had a goalie coach. But the absence of an instructor did nothing to deter young Hasek from pursuing his goal—if anything, it made him work harder to achieve it. Hasek turned himself into both student and teacher, and became the consummate self-taught athlete. "When I was 10 or 11," recalls Hasek, "I'd go and watch the practice of the junior team. And I'd just pay attention to what the goalie was doing and think about it. I'd look for things that worked and for things that didn't. And then I'd try it all out in my practices."

Year	Team	Lea	REGULAR SEASON								PLAYOFFS						
			GP	W	L	T	Mins	GA	SO	Avg	GP	W	L	Mins	GA	SO	Avg
1981-82	Pardubice	Czech	12	....	....	....	661	34	....	3.09	....	....	....	....	....	....	....
1982-83	Pardubice	Czech	42	....	....	....	2358	105	....	2.67	....	....	....	....	....	....	....
1983-84	Pardubice	Czech	40	....	....	....	2304	108	....	2.81	....	....	....	....	....	....	....
1984-85	Pardubice	Czech	42	....	....	....	2419	131	....	3.25	....	....	....	....	....	....	....
1985-86	Pardubice	Czech	45	....	....	....	2689	138	....	3.08	....	....	....	....	....	....	....
1986-87	Pardubice	Czech	43	....	....	....	2515	103	....	2.46	....	....	....	....	....	....	....
1987-88	Pardubice	Czech	31	....	....	....	1862	93	....	3.00	....	....	....	....	....	....	....
1988-89	Pardubice	Czech	42	....	....	....	2507	114	....	2.73	....	....	....	....	....	....	....
1989-90	Dukla Jihlava	Czech	40	....	....	....	2251	80	....	2.13	....	....	....	....	....	....	....
1990-91	Chicago	NHL	5	3	0	1	195	8	0	2.46	3	0	0	69	3	0	2.61
	Indianapolis	IHL	33	20	11	1	1903	80	5	2.52	1	1	0	60	3	0	3.00
1991-92	Chicago	NHL	20	10	4	1	1014	44	1	2.60	3	0	2	158	8	0	3.04
	Indianapolis	IHL	20	7	10	3	1162	69	1	3.56	....	....	....	....	....	....	....
1992-93	Buffalo	NHL	28	11	10	4	1429	75	0	3.15	1	1	0	45	1	0	1.33
1993-94	Buffalo	NHL	58	30	20	6	3358	109	7	1.95	7	3	4	484	13	2	1.61
1994-95	Pardubice	Czech	2	....	....	....	124	6	0	2.90	....	....	....	....	....	....	....
	Buffalo	NHL	41	19	14	7	2416	85	5	2.11	5	1	4	309	18	0	3.50
1995-96	Buffalo	NHL	59	22	30	6	3417	161	2	2.83	....	....	....	....	....	....	....
1996-97	Buffalo	NHL	67	37	20	10	4037	153	5	2.27	3	1	1	153	5	0	1.96
1997-98	Buffalo	NHL	72	33	23	13	4220	147	13	2.09	15	10	5	948	32	1	2.03
1998-99	Buffalo	NHL	64	30	18	14	3817	119	9	1.87	19	13	6	1217	36	2	1.77

Ron Tugnutt

31 OTTAWA SENATORS

It isn't always easy getting used to being a star—especially when you've been someone else's understudy for much of your career.

Take Ron Tugnutt. For the longest time, the kid from Scarborough, Ontario was known as the stand-in, the backup, the perennial No. 2.

But a few years back, as regulars to Ottawa's Corel Centre well know, something started to change. Tugnutt not only began to look like a top-rate goaltender. He began to look like one of the best in the league.

This season, Tugnutt proved that he was. By season end, he'd recorded a save percentage of .925 and a staggering goals against average of 1.79. Not bad for a fellow who was drafted 81st overall by Quebec in the 1986 NHL entry draft. Not bad for a guy who was playing in the minors just three years ago, and was about to head to Europe when then-Senators General Manager Pierre Gauthier gave him a call.

For the longest time, Tugnutt was hardly able to keep his suitcase unpacked. After posting a 12-29-10 record with Quebec in 1990–91, he headed to minor-league Halifax, then to Edmonton, to Anaheim, to Montreal, then back to the minors

in Portland, Maine. Anyone else might have felt like throwing in the pads.

But in Tugnutt's case, the trip was worth the fare. Before he was signed with Ottawa, he played one more season with Portland in the AHL, and that was when something happened.

"I found out how to win again when I went to the AHL," says Tugnutt. "I look at that year as a turning point. I was a little scared in the past on nights when I'd be playing, or maybe intimidated is a better word."

The first year with Ottawa, Tugnutt posted a record of 17-15-1 and a GAA below 3.00 for the first time in his nine-year career. The next year the numbers were also startling. And this season, of course, they were downright unbelievable.

"I'm finally in the right place at the right time," says the guy they call Tugger. "It took a long time to get here."

It is, it seems, the classic tale of the little engine that could.

Still, you can't help getting the feeling that the easygoing father of two is still adjusting to his celebrity status. This, after all, is a netminder who's not inclined to take credit, even when credit is clearly due.

"I'm a firm believer that the goalie doesn't steal the game," he says. "When we play well, we win as a team and we lose as a team."

Last January, when Tugnutt was named as a late replacement to the NHL's North American All-Star team, substituting for an injured Curtis Joseph, Tugnutt seemed more excited about meeting hockey's superstars than being named as one himself.

"I'm seriously looking forward to sitting in the same room as Wayne Gretzky," he said before the game. "I'm looking forward to hav-

ing an all-star jersey and as soon as it's over, I'm going to get everybody to sign it."

These days, it's Tugnutt who's the target of the autograph hounds. Over the past three years, Tugnutt—along with fellow netminder Damian Rhodes—helped transform the Senators into one of the top-ranked teams in the National Hockey League. Rhodes, who split the goaltending duties with Tugnutt almost equally, has now moved south to tend nets for the brand-new Atlanta Thrashers, but Tugnutt is more than happy to be staying put.

> "I'm a firm believer that the goalie doesn't steal the game. When we play well, we win as a team and we lose as a team."

Seems he's pulled up stakes so many times in his hockey career, he's finally thrilled to find a place to call home.

"This is where I see myself finishing my career and living after I'm finished playing," Tugnutt says. "I'll be 32 this year and if things keep on going the way they are I can see playing until I'm 36 maybe.

"This is where I want to be. I've never liked renting, never liked owing someone and not owning. This is the first time I've felt comfortable and confident enough to buy a home where I was playing."

These days, home to Tugnutt, wife Lisa and sons Matt and Jacob is in a new development in the community of Stittsville, just outside Ottawa. Finally, after floating all over the continent, Ron Tugnutt has not only achieved the dream, he's also come to appreciate the road he travelled to find it.

"I think that you go through a lot of adversity, but I'm a firm believer that it just makes you stronger," he says. "Although you go through tough times, it makes the good times that much better."

There was a time, not surprisingly, when Ron Tugnutt was forced to seriously consider life as something other than a goaltender. After all, he'd spent years moving from one team to another, and it sometimes felt as though a future with the National Hockey League was nothing more than a pipe dream. Tugnutt weighed his options, and arrived at the possibility. "I thought about being a fireman," he says. "I was hoping a fire department might need a goaltender for its team. But there were hang-ups—I'm color-blind, partially deaf and claustrophobic." Lucky for Tugnutt, then, that he never had to a take a stab at Career Option No. 2. Turns out he's a heck of a lot more comfortable with ice than with fire.

				REGULAR SEASON								PLAYOFFS					
Year	Team	Lea	GP	W	L	T	Mins	GA	SO	Avg	GP	W	L	Mins	GA	SO	Avg
1984-85	Peterborough	OHL	18	7	4	2	938	59	0	3.77	....	....	....	....	....	....	....
1985-86	Peterborough	OHL	26	18	7	0	1543	74	1	2.88	3	2	0	133	6	0	2.71
1986-87	Peterborough	OHL	31	21	7	2	1891	88	2	2.79	6	3	3	374	21	1	3.37
1987-88	Quebec	NHL	6	2	3	0	284	16	0	3.38	....	....	....	....	....	....	....
	Fredericton Exp	AHL	34	20	9	4	1964	118	1	3.60	4	1	2	204	11	0	3.24
1988-89	Quebec	NHL	26	10	10	3	1367	82	0	3.60	....	....	....	....	....	....	....
	Halifax	AHL	24	14	7	2	1368	79	1	3.46	....	....	....	....	....	....	....
1989-90	Quebec	NHL	35	5	24	3	1978	152	0	4.61	....	....	....	....	....	....	....
	Halifax	AHL	6	1	5	0	366	23	0	3.77	....	....	....	....	....	....	....
1990-91	Quebec	NHL	56	12	29	10	3144	212	0	4.05	....	....	....	....	....	....	....
	Halifax	AHL	2	0	1	0	100	8	0	4.80	....	....	....	....	....	....	....
1991-92	Quebec	NHL	30	6	17	3	1583	106	1	4.02	....	....	....	....	....	....	....
	Halifax	AHL	8	3	3	1	447	30	0	4.03	....	....	....	....	....	....	....
	Edmonton	NHL	3	1	1	0	124	10	0	4.84	2	0	0	60	3	0	3.00
1992-93	Edmonton	NHL	26	9	12	2	1338	93	0	4.17	....	....	....	....	....	....	....
	Canada	WC-A	4	....	....	....	125	6	....	2.87	....	....	....	....	....	....	....
1993-94	Anaheim	NHL	28	10	15	1	1520	76	1	3.00	....	....	....	....	....	....	....
	Montreal	NHL	8	2	3	1	378	24	0	3.81	1	0	1	59	5	0	5.08
1994-95	Montreal	NHL	7	1	3	1	346	18	0	3.12	....	....	....	....	....	....	....
1995-96	Portland	AHL	58	21	23	6	3068	171	2	3.34	13	7	6	782	36	1	2.76
1996-97	Ottawa	NHL	37	17	15	1	1991	93	3	2.80	7	3	4	425	14	1	1.98
1997-98	Ottawa	NHL	42	15	14	8	2236	84	3	2.25	2	0	1	74	6	0	4.86
1998-99	Ottawa	NHL	43	22	10	8	2508	75	3	1.79	2	0	2	118	6	0	3.05

Olaf Kolzig

37 WASHINGTON CAPITALS

There was a time, long before he answered to Godzilla, long before folks called him Olie the Goalie, when Olaf Kolzig did not play goal.

He was a kid. He played both forward and defense and he had little, if any, interest in standing between the pipes. Then one day, the goaltender on his Toronto minor league team didn't show up for a game and Kolzig volunteered to be the stand-in. The rest, as it goes, is history.

His team won that day and Kolzig became the hero.

To the Washington Capitals, he still is.

Kolzig, who at six-foot-three and 225 pounds is one of the goaltending heavyweights in the National Hockey League, became part of the Capitals organization in 1989 when he was selected as Washington's first choice in the Entry Draft. He'd been spotted tending the Western Hockey League nets for the Tri-City Americans, where in 1988–89 he had a record of 16-10-2, and the Caps had liked what they'd seen.

Still, Kolzig did not make an immediate move to Washington. First, he went to work in the AHL, for Baltimore, and later to Hampton Roads of the East Coast Hockey League. It wasn't the NHL, but looking back, Kolzig knows the experience was tremendous. "Hampton was probably the best thing for me," he says.

Over the next four years, Kolzig split duty between the NHL and the AHL, where in 1994 he was awarded the Jack Butterfield Trophy as MVP of the Calder Cup playoffs by posting a 12-5 record and 2.55 goals-against average to lead Portland to the championship.

Kolzig, who is German by parentage, was born in Johannesburg, South Africa, 29 years ago. At the age of four, he moved to Canada with his family, living first in Edmonton, then Toronto, then Halifax, then eventually in the tiny seaside community of Union Bay, British Columbia, which Kolzig describes as "the most beautiful spot on earth."

Olie the Goalie

Kolzig grew up idolizing Patrick Roy, but never imagined himself playing in the same league as his hero. He thought he'd only scale the ladder to the junior level, then perhaps pursue a career in sports medicine.

But things didn't turn out that way. The scouts started to take notice of the big goaltender, and so did the Washington Capitals.

Still, it wasn't until the 1998 Stanley Cup finals, when the Capitals entered hockey's greatest duel with the Detroit Red Wings, that much of the hockey world was formally introduced to Olaf Kolzig. Until then, Olie the Goalie didn't see an awful lot of action with the Caps. He seemed permanently relegated to the No. 2 position, perennially working as the backup to Vezina Trophy winner Jim Carey, and later to the 1990 Cup winner Bill Ranford.

Then, however, everything changed. Ranford became injured during the 1997–98 season and Kolzig was called into duty.

It was quite a coming-out. The history books will record that the Wings took the series and won the hardware, but Kolzig emerged as a sensation in his own right. Godzilla, who won 11 of his first 15 playoff games, demonstrated to everyone who watched that he was a player who gave his all whenever he wore the pads.

Back in Union Bay, where Kolzig's parents manage a general store, the town of 1,400 was going crazy. Kolzig's folks were pursued for interviews and his mother was busy selling postcards she'd made that read "Home of Olie the Goalie."

"During the playoffs, she created an Olie the Goalie mannequin in the store and always posted the results of our games on the bulletin board," recalls Kolzig.

Olie's performance may have woken up the

sleepy little town, but it didn't come as a surprise to the folks who'd known Kolzig for any length of time. One of those people is Dan Donaldson, director of marketing for the Tri-City Americans, with whom Kolzig had played in the late 1980s.

Funnily, he doesn't gush on about Kolzig's playing ability. He'd rather praise the man.

"Olie is very special people, a total class act," says Donaldson. "We feel very privileged, thrilled to say he played here."

> "Now I'm starting to play more of a consistent style, butterflying on everything, and when you do that, you automatically take the five-hole away. I sometimes still get beat, but not quite as much. "

Kolzig, who'll go down in the Tri-City history books as first WHL goalie to ever score a goal, back on Nov. 29, 1989, is an athlete with remarkable agility and speed, given his size.

"When I came out of junior, I was playing more of a Ron Hextall-type style—standing up, going down at different times," says Kolzig. "Now I'm starting to play more of a consistent style, butterflying on everything, and when you do that, you automatically take the five-hole away. I sometimes still get beat, but not quite as much."

Kolzig is the consummate physical athlete, but he's also recognized as a player with a steady mental attitude. He takes it easy, one game at a time, and works on staying as calm as he can.

"As a goalie," he says, "if you try to think too much and overplay situations too much, you get yourself into trouble. I just want to go out there and react. I think the biggest thing for goaltenders is just to be confident and play big."

Last season, too, the big guy continued to be big. Washington didn't make the playoffs, but Kolzig ended up in fine form, posting a .900 save percentage and a goals-against average of 2.58.

Not bad at all for a guy who spent almost a decade with the Washington Capitals before becoming No. 1. He may be a self-described late bloomer, but the Capitals don't really care. They just know that he bloomed, and that's all that really matters.

The Tri-Cities Coliseum in Kennewick, Washington will always have a special place in Olaf Kolzig's memory. That's where he became the first WHL goaltender to score a goal, back in November 1989 when the Tri-City Americans took on Seattle. "In all honesty, all I really wanted to do was sort of lob it over everybody, but it was a line drive," recalls Kolzig." It actually went through one of the Seattle player's legs, then right down the middle into the net." To say Kolzig is a hero in Kennewick is somewhat of an understatement: In 1998, several thousand showed up at the arena to see his No. 33 jersey retired.

			REGULAR SEASON								PLAYOFFS						
Year	Team	Lea	GP	W	L	T	Mins	GA	SO	Avg	GP	W	L	Mins	GA	SO	Avg
1987-88	New Westmin.	WHL	15	6	5	0	650	48	1	4.43	3	0	3	149	11	0	4.43
1988-89	Tri-City	WHL	30	16	10	2	1671	97	1	3.48	....	....	....	....	....	....	....
1989-90	Washington	Fr Tour	2	....	....	....	65	4	....	3.69	....	....	....	....	....	....	....
	Washington	NHL	2	0	2	0	120	12	0	6.00	....	....	....	....	....	....	....
	Tri-City	WHL	48	27	27	3	2504	250	1	4.38	6	4	0	318	27	0	5.09
1990-91	Baltimore	AHL	26	10	12	1	1367	72	0	3.16	....	....	....	....	....	....	....
	Hampton	ECHL	21	11	9	1	1248	71	2	3.41	3	1	2	180	14	0	4.66
1991-92	Baltimore	AHL	28	5	17	2	1503	105	1	4.19	....	....	....	....	....	....	....
	Hampton	ECHL	14	11	3	0	847	41	0	2.90	....	....	....	....	....	....	....
1992-93	Washington	NHL	1	0	0	0	20	2	0	6.00	....	....	....	....	....	....	....
	Rochester	AHL	49	25	16	4	2737	168	0	3.68	17	9	8	1040	61	0	3.52
1993-94	Washington	NHL	7	0	3	0	224	20	0	5.36	....	....	....	....	....	....	....
	Portland	AHL	29	16	8	5	1725	88	3	3.06	17	12	5	1035	44	0	2.55
1994-95	Washington	NHL	14	2	8	2	724	30	0	2.49	2	1	0	44	1	0	1.36
	Portland	AHL	2	1	0	1	125	3	0	1.44	....	....	....	....	....	....	....
1995-96	Washington	NHL	18	4	8	2	897	46	0	3.08	5	2	3	341	11	0	1.94
	Portland	AHL	5	5	0	0	300	7	1	1.40	....	....	....	....	....	....	....
1996-97	Germany	W Cup	1	....	....	....	45	5	0	6.67	....	....	....	....	....	....	....
	Washington	NHL	29	8	15	4	1645	71	2	2.59	....	....	....	....	....	....	....
	Germany	WC-A	4	0	3	0	199	13	0	3.92	....	....	....	....	....	....	....
1997-98	Washington	NHL	64	33	18	10	3788	139	5	2.20	21	12	9	1351	44	4	1.95
	Germany	Olympics	2	2	0	0	120	2	1	1.00	....	....	....	....	....	....	....
1998-99	Washington	NHL	64	26	31	3	3586	154	4	2.58	....	....	....	....	....	....	....

History

They are, by any estimation, a peculiar brand of athlete. There they stand: in front of a net six feet wide and four feet high, waiting to be assaulted, again and again. Waiting, not fearfully, but eagerly.

They're there, anticipating the slapshots and the one-timers, the rebounds and the wrap-arounds, not because they have to, but because that's exactly where they want to be.

Peculiar, yes. But there's also something undeniably mysterious about the men who strap the padding to their shins and do everything they can, turning cartwheels if necessary, to keep their cage a puck-free zone. Hockey's guardians may wear the team uniform and bear the team name, but in many ways, they're playing a game all their own. A game called goaltending.

It's a game, they'll all tell you, that's as exhilarating as it is terrifying, as electrifying as it is nerve-wracking. "The only job worse," the legendary Gump Worsley once said, "is a javelin catcher at a track-and-field meet."

They came to it by different roads. At one time, they might have been plunked in front of the net simply because they couldn't skate fast enough to be a winger or a forward.

Some, like the legendary Johnny Bower, were handed the goalie stick as kids because no one else wanted it. Others, like Gerry Cheevers, got the job because the goaltender didn't show, and because someone had to wear the pads.

In Chris Osgood's case, it wasn't a default position, it was something he actively pursued. He liked the feeling he got when he made a terrific save. He also liked being the guy who led the team onto the ice.

For others, it was inspiration, pure and simple, that made goaltending seem like the best job. Nikolai Khabibulin identified his hero early on, and decided he wanted to follow in the footsteps of Vladislav Tretiak.

Martin Brodeur had his hero: Patrick Roy. And Patrick Roy had his too, Quebec Nordiques netminder Daniel Bouchard. So devoted was the young Roy to his personal idol that he slept with his hero's hockey stick.

But the dreams were not always instantly achievable. As any goaltender in the National Hockey League well knows, it's one thing to have a childhood goal, and quite another to achieve it.

There are hurdles, legions of them. Maybe your family can't afford the equipment, so you have to improvise, like the young Johnny Bower did, by strapping pieces of mattress to his shins, and later, Eaton's catalogues.

You want the dream, you do what it takes. And if you're Dominik Hasek and you're a six-year-old growing up in Pardubice in the Czech Republic, you do what seems obvious when you don't own skates. You screw blades to the bottoms of your shoes.

And then, of course, you go to work. You practice. And you practice. And then, if you decide you still want it more than anything else, you go out and practice some more.

Then, if you're lucky, someone will notice the way your glove hand is lightning fast, or the way you can poke-check with more speed and agility than anyone else in a goalie mask, or the way you can drop to a butterfly as fast as a bullet. Someone, if you're lucky, will notice that

you're not only guarding your net. You're also keeping it empty.

There are hurdles, waves of them, that separate the boy with the dream from the man in the National Hockey League. But for a select few, they are leapable. These are the goalies who are not only able to deflect the assault, but who, love the battle the most.

....

As long as there has been a game called hockey, there's been someone positioned in front of the net to watch for speeding pucks. But while the goaltender's function hasn't changed a whit—he's still the last line of defense on the

Sawchuk also wore a goalie make, but not before he needed more than 400 stitches to knit together virtually every part of his face, from lip to eye, from hairline to eyebrow.

ice—his style has changed considerably.

Terry Sawchuk would no doubt be a little miffed if he could see Ed Belfour play a game today. To begin with, he just looks so much different than Sawchuk and his gang of '50s goalies, Jacques Plante and Glenn Hall, Johnny Bower and Gump Worsley.

For starters, he wears a mask. Sure, Plante did as well, but only after he'd taken a backhander in the nose back in November of 1959,

and fell to the ice, blood gushing from his wound. And yes, Worsley wore one too, but only for six of 860 regular season games and another 70 playoff contests.

True, Sawchuk also wore a goalie mask, but not before he needed more than 400 stitches to knit together virtually every part of his face, from lip to eye, from hairline to eyebrow.

Today, Belfour would probably be more inclined to put his skates on the wrong feet than head onto the ice without a face mask. Like all of his contemporaries, he dresses both for optimum performance and optimum protection. And that, not surprisingly, affects the way he plays.

Today's goalies stand like knights in shining armor. They wear not only masks, but padding that's lighter and more insulating than that worn by their early brothers. Naturally then, they're able to focus less on survival and more on stopping the puck, and are more inclined—even eager—to jump into a scramble headfirst, and to use their masks as yet another means of deflecting the puck.

Their costumes have changed, and so has their make-up. Today's goaltenders must train relentlessly and be uncompromisingly conditioned, both physically and mentally. They should be able to skate like the wind and react on a dime—and think faster than they can move.

"Goaltenders today are athletes, which wasn't universal years ago," says Ian Clark, director of the Goaltenders Development Institute.

Perhaps, then, if there's one thing about goaltending that was never changed at all, it's that the man who straps on the pads, game after game, has always been the toughest in the game.

"There's no question today's top goaltenders have all the attributes one wants in a high-performance athlete: technical skills, physical ability, emotional and psychological management, and intelligence."

And there's no question that they need all those attributes. After all, the pucks are flying faster, the forwards are skating quicker. The game has become more intense, more demanding, than it has ever been before.

But if the other players are involved in a different brand of hockey—one that's swifter and sharper and so hugely adored by the fans—so, too, are the guardians.

For one thing, they do things, amazing things, that their predecessors would have considered unthinkable. Today's goalies will do anything humanly possible to keep the puck from the net: they'll dive out of the crease to make the impossible save, they'll drop to the butterfly in an instant or thrust out their glove to make an unfathomable rapid-fire snatch. At one time, however, hockey's guardians were a lot less acrobatic, partly because of their vulnerability, and partly because of the rules of the game.

Used to be that a goaltender worked stand-up. But when Clint Benedict appeared on the scene, back in the 1917–1918 season, the rule-makers realized they had a problem on their hands. The legendary Benedict, who eventually went down in history as the first netminder to wear a mask, if only for a single game at the end of his 13-year career, was a sprawler by nature and was fond of dropping to the ice to stop the puck.

> At one time, hockey's guardians were a lot less acrobatic, partly because of their vulnerability, and partly because of the rules of the game.

Longest shutout sequence by a goaltender:
Alex Connell - 461 minutes, 29 seconds

Most wins by a goaltender, career:
Terry Sawchuk - 447

Most wins by a goaltender, one season:
Bernie Parent - 47

Longest winning streak by a goaltender, one season:
Gilles Gilbert - 17

Longest undefeated streak by a goaltender, one season:
Gerry Cheevers - 32 games

Longest undefeated streak by a goaltender in his first NHL season:
Grant Fuhr - 23 games

But that was against the rules, and goalies who went down to make saves were assessed minor penalties. The NHL's precursor, the National Hockey Association, even had a rule that hit goalies in their pocketbooks: it levied a $2 fine every time they fell to the ice.

The rules, however, seemed made to be broken. When it was realized that it would have been difficult—if not impossible—to penalize Benedict every time he sprawled on the ice, it was decided that the rulebook would be rewritten and that all goalies would be allowed to fall, sit or even lie down on the ice without being reprimanded.

And so, a new type of goalie emerged, one who tended to become increasingly flexible as the decades progressed. Now, of course, the typical goaltender not only goes up and down like a yo-yo — he'll even stand on his head if he's able.

But as Detroit Red Wings' captain Steve Yzerman points out, the changes didn't come overnight.

"Goalies were stand-up for the most part 10 years ago, and a lot of shots along the ice and through the screens would go in," he recalls. "You don't see as many easy goals now because goalies are comfortable with going down, laying their sticks on the ice and taking away the bottom-half of the net."

But there are also other things, other now-routine aspects of goaltending that would strike the game's forefathers as a tad peculiar, if not downright insane. Today, for instance, goalies are taught not to stay deep in the crease when an opponent is barreling toward them down the ice, but to move out of the

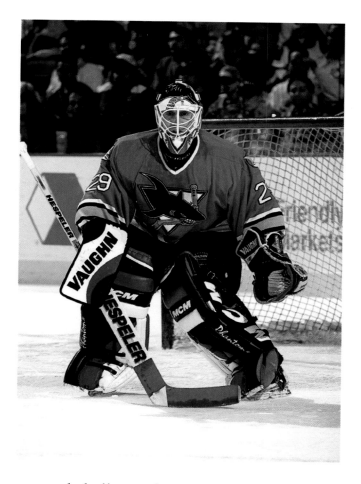

net and challenge the enemy, one-on-one.

Contemporary guardians not only move out in front of the net, they also move beside it and even behind it, something that would have seemed mighty peculiar to anybody preceding seven-time Vezina Trophy winner Jacques Plante.

It was the innovative Plante, after all, who not only popularized the use of the face mask, but who also introduced the concept of the roving goaltender, a hockey player who not only guarded the crease, but left it periodically to pass the puck to a teammate.

Onlookers thought it astonishing. Today, it's standard practice.

The job description has changed, no question about it. And yes, it has been a change for the better.

"The standard of goaltending has never been

this good," says former goaltender Kelly Hrudey, now a hockey commentator. "At least not in my time. When I came into the league [in 1984] a lot of teams had goaltending problems. Every team is getting good goaltending nowadays."

One of the reasons why things have improved is because the goalie coach has entered the picture. He hasn't been there for long, but he's definitely making an impact.

For the most part, the NHL's goalie coaches are themselves former goalies, and for that reason, they have a special understanding of the challenges—and the enormous pressures—faced by the men in the crease.

Still, ask anyone who guards the posts for a National Hockey League team, and you'll probably hear a story about a kid who taught himself.

"For the most part, most goalies don't get much direction on the minor-league level," says Clark of the Goaltenders Development Institute. "Here we have this position that's so valuable, and yet so many of them have pretty much learned it on their own. How do they do that? They have to be the hardest workers on the ice and the most focused."

And in many cases, they are. John Vanbiesbrouck didn't go to goalie school when he was a kid, and neither did Ron Hextall. As for Dominik Hasek, well, he didn't have a goalie coach either. He just went out and watched the other guys, the older ones, and then he'd try their moves himself.

To say they're hard working is putting it mildly.

Make it to the world of NHL goaltending and

Now, of course, the typical goaltender not only goes up and down like a yo-yo — he'll even stand on his head if he's able.

you're far more than a diligent worker. In many ways, you're also super-human. "Nobody understands the position who hasn't played it," former goalie John Garrett once said. "Hockey is like a team game, but for a goalie, it's more like an individual sport."

Indeed it is. It's a sport where you can be a hero one minute and a villain the next. Make an error as a forward and the crowds may never know, but do the same as a goalie and the light will flash, the horns will sound, and the opposition will start to celebrate.

"Only a goalie cannot make mistakes," said the great Russian netminder, Vladislav Tretiak, "because his mistakes mean goals."

It is, suggests Olaf Kolzig of the Washington Capitals, the toughest position of any in organized sport.

Perhaps, then, if there's one thing about goaltending that has never changed at all, it's exactly that: that the man who straps on the pads, game after game, has always been the toughest on the ice.

Today's goaltending fraternity, that exclusive brotherhood that's comprised of the likes of Patrick Roy and Martin Brodeur, Byron Dafoe and Curtis Joseph, is undeniably indomitable. But so, too, were the guardians who came before them: men like Georges Vezina, after whom goaltending's greatest prize is named, and Glenn Hall, who tended the nets in an amazing 502 consecutive games, and Terry Sawchuk, who recorded a staggering 103 career shutouts.

There were others, of course, people with names like Gump Worsley and Bill Durnan, Bernie Parent and Rogie Vachon, Ken Dryden and Tony Esposito. They may have belonged to different eras and they may have registered different accomplishments, but they've all enjoyed considerable success.

For one thing, they've all been made aware of the stereotype, that age-old notion that anyone who'd ever stand in front of a hockey net had something wrong with his faculties.

"Yeah," says Philadelphia's John Vanbiesbrouck, "to be a goalie, first you have to remove half your brain."

He is, of course, laughing.

In truth, the stereotype couldn't be farther from the truth. Sure, some goalies may be quirky, some may be a tad eccentric, and some may even have their superstitions. But the reality is, if you make it as a guardian in the National Hockey League, you're not only going to be in top physical condition, you're also going to be in top mental shape. How else would you be able to read every pass on the ice, to anticipate every turn, every play, every shot?

It may, in the end, be impossible for the rest of us to comprehend, but at least goalies understand. Some may call them lunatics, but when it comes to goaltending, there's one truth that's undeniable: the man who guards the net knows the true definition of excitement.

"I think the job of being a goaltender is the biggest high you could possibly have," says Ron Tugnutt. "People say the guys who play goal are crazy to do what we do, but I've always had the feeling that I was the smart one, because everyone else was chasing the puck, and I just stood there and waited for it."

> "People say the guys who play goal are crazy to do what we do, but I've always had the feeling that I was the smart one, because everyone else was chasing the puck, and I just stood there and waited for it."

Eddie Belfour

20 · DALLAS STARS

Ed Belfour likes to stay in shape.

That, as anyone who's familiar with the Dallas Stars netminder well knows, is like saying ice is cold. Ed Belfour doesn't just value fitness. You could probably say he's obsessed with it.

There are no less than 12 different exercises that Belfour works on, two times every day. He has a salt water pool in his home and a contingent of massage therapists.

Off-season, he doesn't pack the routine away with the skates. He continues to work out a minimum of two hours a day.

"Belfour is a real workhorse," Detroit Red Wings' star Brendan Shanahan has observed. "I know that he is a fitness fanatic and likes to stay in shape to handle the heavy workload. He is an extremely competitive person."

Competitive, yes, and intense, and determined. The Eagle, as he's known to his adoring fans at Reunion Arena, is tenacity personified. He's an athlete who can't stand the thought of losing, and will do whatever it takes to prevent that from happening.

In Belfour's case, that means being 100 percent prepared for every single game. As any of Belfour's buddies can testify, he is your consummate details guy, a goalie who has some of the most intricate pre-game rituals of any professional athlete.

On game days, he'll eat the same

thing: either steak or salmon. He'll sleep for two hours, then head to the rink where he'll check out his sticks, have a rubdown, do some exercises, have a meeting, then exercise some more. The routine is the same every time, right down to the millisecond.

Star's center Guy Carbonneau says it's nothing short of mind-boggling. "I know goalies are different," he says, "but if I had to do everything he has to do to get ready for one game, I would have quit 10 years ago."

But as Belfour sees it, the prep work really does what he wants it to do: it helps him get set for the game.

"I try to keep it the exact same way all the time," says the 34-year-old native of Carman, Manitoba. "It's a positive routine I've acquired through the years. I do it, and I'm ready to kick some butt."

So meticulous is Belfour, and so preoccupied with his equipment, that he's been known to spend six hours at the sharpener trying to get the perfect edge for his skates. He had a think-tank devote three days to developing the design for his latest mask. He spends entire days at equipment factories.

"Equipment is something I need to feel good about," he says. "If I have a chance to do anything to make myself more prepared, more ready to have a good game, I'm going to do it."

If all this demonstrates anything, it's that Belfour is utterly committed to the job at hand. It's that very commitment, that do-or-die attitude, that's always kept Belfour focused on the ultimate goal, even when the odds of achieving it seemed not at all encouraging.

Belfour didn't become a goaltender until he was 12, and only then because no one else wanted the job. In high school, he was cut from the team for three years, until he was a senior. He played basketball instead, but ended up fouling out of every game he played.

He continued to play hockey but was never drafted by a team, neither major-junior nor NHL.

It would have discouraged most folks, but not Eddie Belfour.

"You'll never find a more competitive, determined person," says Jeff Friesen, Belfour's longtime friend and fellow car-racing nut. "That's how he got to where he is—with people telling him he can't do things and then proving them wrong."

Belfour has proven the critics wrong time and time again. Way back in 1986–87, say, when he posted a 29-4-0 record with North Dakota of the WCHA, or the following year, when he went 32-25-0 with Saginaw of the IHL, or in any of his subsequent seasons with the Chicago Blackhawks, who had signed him as a free agent back in 1987.

In just one season 1990–91—he posted 43 wins, breaking Tony Esposito's previous Blackhawk record of 38. In another—1992–93—he led in shutouts, with seven, and posted 41 wins to become one of only five NHL goalies to win more than 40 games in a season.

His awards would make the critics eat their words. Belfour, who wears the number 20 in honor of the great Russian goaltender Vladislav Tretiak, his goalie coach in Chicago, is a two-time winner of the Vezina Trophy, awarded the league's top goalie, and a three-time recipient of the Jennings Trophy, handed to the team that has the lowest goals-against average. He won the Calder Trophy in 1991 as NHL rookie

of the year, and is a two-time first team all-star.

In 1997–98, his first season with the Stars, Belfour recorded the National Hockey League's best goals-against average—an amazing 1.88—and this year he piloted Dallas to the 1999 Stanley Cup Championship.

Belfour would call the Stars' first Cup victory, the finest moment in his hockey career. In a head-to-head battle with Dominik Hasek, Belfour seemed to get stronger as the series went on, culminating in the dramatic win in overtime in the sixth game.

"This is the greatest feeling in the world," said Belfour, who throughout his career had heard the critic's whispers that he was no good under playoff pressure. I hope this silences all those people who said I'd never be able to do this."

Ed Belfour has arrived, no matter how you look at it. But even though his on-ice successes are apparent to anyone who's paid even passing attention, there's more to this man when he leaves the rink.

The Eagle—he was handed the nickname back in his stellar rookie season with Chicago—does not simply give his all to hockey. He also gives generously to those who are less fortunate than he, specifically to children who are battling life-threatening illnesses.

Five years ago, Belfour became involved with the Make-a-Wish Foundation, an organization that grants special wishes to sick children. He has organized a golf tournament to benefit the foundation, and regularly buys tickets for children and their families in the "Eagle's Nest" section of Reunion Arena. Belfour

> "That's how he got to where he is—with people telling him he can't do things and then proving them wrong."

even has the foundation's symbol—a wishbone with a ribbon tied to the top—painted on his goalie mask.

Belfour's other off-ice interest—car-racing—is almost as old as his love for hockey.

The Eagle developed a passion for fast cars when he was growing up, and began racing them when he was 18.

"Drag racing is a huge adrenaline rush," says Belfour, who has a growing automobile collection and has competed in races throughout Ohio, Indiana and Michigan, clocking speeds of up to 170 miles an hour.

It is, it seems, just another indication that Ed Belfour is not your average guy-next-door. There's nothing, in fact, that's average about this hockey guardian, and that's just fine with the folks down in Dallas.

"I don't like to lose," says Belfour. "I'm a competitive person. That's who I am. I'm not going to change."

Ed Belfour has been playing goal for eons, but he's also taken a turn at forward—as recently as last season. Belfour scored a couple of goals in a pickup game involving 25 of his buddies at Toronto's Maple Leafs Gardens, just before the Leafs were about to move out of the legendary rink. Belfour wanted his friends to have a chance to play in the building before the Leafs left, so he paid $1,000 for 90 minutes of play. The guys, including a furniture maker, a construction worker, and several mechanics from as far away as Dallas, Chicago and Detroit, had the time of their lives. "It was a blast," says Belfour. "We had two teams. Some guys drove. Some guys flew. We all made it and had jerseys made up. We took photographs and had a great time. It was a dream come true for a lot of guys who hadn't been there."

Year	Team	Lea	GP	W	L	T	Mins	GA	SO	Avg	GP	W	L	Mins	GA	SO	Avg
							REGULAR SEASON						PLAYOFFS				
1986-87	Uni North Dakota	WCHA	34	29	4	0	2049	81	3	2.43	....	....	....	....	....	....	....
1987-88	Saginaw	IHL	61	32	25	0	3446	183	3	3.19	9	4	5	561	33	0	3.53
1988-89	Chicago	NHL	23	4	12	3	1148	74	0	3.87	....	....	....	....	....	....	....
	Saginaw	IHL	29	12	10	0	1760	92	0	3.10	5	2	3	298	14	0	2.82
1989-90	Canada	Nat-Team	33	13	12	6	1808	93	0	3.08	....	....	....	....	....	....	....
	Chicago	NHL	....	....	....	....	....	....	....	....	9	4	2	409	17	0	2.49
1990-91	Chicago	NHL	74	43	19	7	4127	170	4	2.47	6	2	4	295	20	0	4.07
1991-92	Canada Cup						DID NOT PLAY - SPARE GOALTENDER										
	Chicago	NHL	52	21	18	10	2928	132	5	2.70	18	12	4	949	39	1	2.47
1992-93	Chicago	NHL	71	41	18	11	4106	177	7	2.59	4	0	4	249	13	0	3.13
1993-94	Chicago	NHL	70	37	24	6	3998	178	7	2.67	6	2	4	360	15	0	2.50
1994-95	Chicago	NHL	42	22	15	3	2450	93	5	2.28	16	9	7	1014	37	1	2.19
1995-96	Chicago	NHL	50	22	17	10	2956	135	1	2.74	9	6	3	666	23	1	2.07
1996-97	Chicago	NHL	33	11	15	6	1966	88	1	2.69	....	....	....	....	....	....	....
	San Jose	NHL	13	3	9	0	757	43	1	3.41	....	....	....	....	....	....	....
1997-98	Dallas	NHL	61	37	12	10	3581	112	9	1.88	17	10	7	1039	31	1	1.79
1998-99	Dallas	NHL	61	35	15	9	3536	117	5	1.99	23	16	7	1544	43	3	1.67

Chris Osgood

30 DETROIT RED WINGS

It was when he was 10 years old that Chris Osgood, a Prairie boy growing up in Medicine Hat, Alberta, decided where he wanted to be positioned on a hockey rink: right in front of the net.

He convinced his parents that he was certain about goaltending. He liked the importance of the position and the feeling he had when he stopped the puck, and he liked being the player who led his team out onto the ice. He watched his father shell out $1,000 for equipment.

Soon afterward, Osgood was sidelined with a minor injury, but he wasn't content to sit for long. He wanted to get back out there as quickly as possible—but this time, as a forward.

His dad was not amused.

"I just said, 'Over my dead body,' says John Osgood. " 'I just spent a thousand dollars on you. You're playing goalie.' "

But Chris, a rather stubborn kid, did exactly what he wanted to: he went out that day and he skated as a forward. And, oh yes, he also happened to score seven goals.

The story, of course, speaks volumes about Chris Osgood. It wasn't that he was confused about his hockey positioning, it's just that he was— and still is—an utterly determined individual.

"Even when he was just a baby, he was very, very stubborn," recalls his father. "We absolutely could never get him to eat. He'd look right at us

51

and dump it on the floor. You could never coax him into anything."

But the qualities that riled his parents are striking his coaches in a completely different way. A stubborn baby may be a bit of pain, but a resolute goaltender is anything but. It's that quality, that drive to persevere, that's landed Osgood where he is today. "I always wanted to be one of the top goalies in the league," he says.

And that's exactly what he is.

In Hockeytown, you want your goaltenders to be tough—which is precisely what Chris Osgood is all about. This, after all, is a guy who claims there was only one occasion when he succumbed to pressure, and it had nothing to do with hockey: It was years ago, when he was in sixth grade and forgot his lines in a skit.

Indeed, the Detroit Red Wings' No. 1 goalie has been recognized not only for his agility, competitiveness and speed, but also for his ability to bounce back after letting in a bad goal. And in a town with a Stanley Cup tradition,

the fans wouldn't expect anything less. As Red Wings' center Kris Draper has observed: "The two toughest jobs in this city are Lions quarterback and Red Wings goalie—and not in that order."

The Wings first spotted Osgood when he was still playing junior hockey in Medicine Hat, a town of about 45,000, three hours east of Calgary. There was much to be impressed about.

Osgood was with the WHL for three seasons, playing with Brandon and Seattle as well as Medicine Hat. He shutout the opposition on seven occasions during that time, and in 1990–91 was named to the WHL's East Second-Team All-Stars.

Osgood became a Red Wing in the 1991 Entry

"Even when he was just a baby, he was very, very stubborn," recalls his father. "We absolutely could never get him to eat. He'd look right at us and dump it on the floor. You could never coax him into anything."

Draft—he was Detroit's third choice—but played a season with the AHL in Adirondack before moving to Hockeytown.

He made his debut in the 1993–94 season, playing in 41 games, winning 23 and securing a 2.86 goals-against average. The next year, when the Red Wings acquired Mike Vernon, Osgood was handed less ice time, but still managed to win 14 of his 19 outings and maintain an average of 2.26.

In 1995–96, Osgood was given a bigger opportunity to showcase his talents. He played in 50 games, recorded 39 wins and recorded a 2.17 average. That year, he was a finalist for the Vezina Trophy, and along with Vernon, was handed the Jennings Trophy for the team with the best goals-against average.

But it was in 1997–98, the year the Red Wings were working to become back-to-back Stanley Cup champions, that Osgood faced his biggest challenge. This time, Osgood was back-up to no one. The previous August, Vernon had left the Wings for San Jose.

It was in the conference finals against Dallas that Osgood faced the greatest pressure. The Wings had hoped to end the series in Game 5, and were on their way to doing exactly that when Stars' forward Guy Carbonneau scored with just 85 seconds remaining. Shortly into overtime, it was Jamie Langenbrunner who scored for the Stars again, forcing a sixth game in Detroit.

The pressure on Osgood was enormous. Described by Detroit GM Ken Holland as an

Described by Detroit GM Ken Holland as an athlete who is "driven to be one of the best," Osgood rose to the occasion that night, and delivered a 2-0 shutout, propelling the Wings into the Stanley Cup final for the second year in a row.

athlete who is "driven to be one of the best," Osgood rose to the occasion that night and delivered a 2-0 shutout, propelling the Wings into the Stanley Cup Finals for the second year in a row.

"That should go down in history. It won't, but it should go down in history as mental toughness at its peak," says hockey analyst and former NHL goalie Kelly Hrudey.

These days, of course, the 26-year-old Osgood, is continuing to prove his No. 1 capabilities. The Red Wings stumbled in last year's playoffs when Osgood was out of the lineup with an injury. When he returned during the western conference semi-finals against Colorado, he wasn't 100 percent and the Avalanche came back from a two-game-to-none deficit to knock off the defending Stanley Cup champions.

But few people doubt Chris Osgood will return to the Stanley Cup finals again before his career is finished. Great goalies somehow just find themselves there.

Where you come from plays a large part in determining where you end up going—and no one knows that better than Chris Osgood. He grew up in a house on 24th Street in Medicine Hat, Alberta, a Prairie town that lives and breathes hockey. It was there that Osgood learned to play the game, and where he eventually tended net for the Western Hockey League's Medicine Hat Tigers, a team whose grads have included Trevor Linden, Craig Berube, Kelly Hrudey, and Jamie Huscroft. "This is a great place to be a kid playing hockey," says Osgood, looking back at his days in Medicine Hat. "Here, you know everybody. It's a fun atmosphere to grow up into the game."

			REGULAR SEASON								PLAYOFFS						
Year	Team	Lea	GP	W	L	T	Mins	GA	SO	Avg	GP	W	L	Mins	GA	SO	Avg
1989-90	Medicine Hat	WHL	57	24	28	2	3094	228	0	4.42	3	0	3	173	17	0	5.91
1990-91	Medicine Hat	WHL	46	23	18	3	2630	173	2	3.95	12	7	5	712	42	0	3.54
1991-92	Medicine Hat	WHL	15	10	3	0	819	44	0	3.22	....	....	....	....	....	....	....
	Brandon	WHL	16	3	10	1	890	60	1	4.04	....	....	....	....	....	....	....
	Seattle	WHL	21	12	7	1	1217	65	1	3.20	15	9	6	904	51	0	3.38
1992-93	Adirondack	AHL	45	19	19	4	2438	159	0	3.91	1	0	1	59	2	0	2.03
1993-94	Detroit	NHL	41	23	8	5	2206	105	2	2.86	6	3	2	307	12	1	2.35
	Adirondack	AHL	4	3	1	0	239	13	0	3.26	....	....	....	....	....	....	....
1994-95	Detroit	NHL	19	14	5	0	1087	41	1	2.26	2	0	0	68	2	0	1.76
	Adirondack	AHL	2	1	1	0	120	6	0	3.00	....	....	....	....	....	....	....
1995-96	Detroit	NHL	50	39	6	5	2933	106	5	2.17	15	8	7	936	33	2	2.12
1996-97	Detroit	NHL	47	23	13	9	2769	106	6	2.30	2	0	0	47	2	0	2.55
1997-98	Detroit	NHL	64	33	20	11	3807	140	6	2.21	22	16	6	1361	48	2	2.12
1998-99	Detroit	NHL	63	34	25	4	3691	149	3	2.42	6	4	2	358	14	1	2.35

Mike Dunham

1 NASHVILLE PREDATORS

Finally, Mike Dunham has found what he's always wanted: a piece of the action.

He couldn't find it on the ballfield—at least, not enough of it—back when he was a kid playing Little League. He couldn't find it on the hockey rink—at least, not enough of it—when he was playing in New Jersey as backup goaltender to Martin Brodeur.

In 1998–99, however, the 26-year-old saw more action than he could ever have imagined. As the starting goalie for the brand-new Nashville Predators, he played 2472 minutes in 44 games, often facing a rapid-fire assault of rubber. Just 14 games into the season he'd faced a staggering 477 shots.

"This is something I wanted," says Dunham, who was drafted in 1990 as New Jersey's fourth selection in the Entry Draft.

As backup to Brodeur for two years, Dunham was handed only the occasional opportunity to step between the pipes—about once every three weeks he figures. "That was the only game I could think about for the next three weeks, whether it was good or bad. Now I'll just play, have fun and do my best."

His best has indeed been impressive. By season end, he'd garnered a goals-against average of 3.08 and a save percentage of .908, mighty remarkable considering the workload.

It was when he was just eight years old that Dunham, a native of Johnson City, New York, first strapped on goalie pads. (He'd given Little League a shot, but found it wasn't fast enough, so he quit after two years.) Dunham tried out for a squirt hockey team, comprised of boys who were two years older, and was accepted, only to discover there wasn't a goaltender.

"Since I was the youngest guy, they asked me if I'd play, and I said I'd give it a try, and here I am . . . still trying."

Trying, and succeeding, as well. Dunham, a big goaltender who stands six-foot-three and weighs 200 pounds, may still be working on things, but he's no longer a journeyman. His resume is proof of that.

For starters, he played three seasons with the University of Maine Black Bears, posting a 41-6-3 career record and leading the team to the 1992–93 NCAA title.

Dunham was a member of the U.S. national

> Dunham, a big goaltender who stands six-foot-three and weighs 200 pounds, may still be working on things, but he's no longer a journeyman.

team from 1991 to 1994, and in 1994 a member of the U.S. Olympic hockey team that traveled to Lillehammer. He turned pro in 1993–94, posting a 20-7-8 record and a 2.80 GAA in his first season with Albany of the AHL, numbers that were good enough to earn Dunham the Harry "Hap" Holmes award for lowest GAA in the league.

His first NHL start came in 1996 when Dunham helped steer the Devils to a win over the Chicago Blackhawks at the United Center. His family was there to watch, in spite of the fact that Dunham hadn't been given enough notice to let them know he'd be playing.

"It was kind of short notice and I couldn't get hold of them," he recalls. "I felt bad thinking that they'd have to watch it on television."

Luckily, his family drove out anyway—"I guess it was Mom's intuition," Dunham says—and caught the entire show.

Certainly, there were other great moments with the Devils, but there also times when he felt frustrated that he was unable to get the ice time he longed for. In two full seasons with New Jersey, Dunham appeared in just 41 of 164 games, playing just 1,800 total minutes. Still, there was an undeniable upside in being able to work as understudy to one of the top netminders in the world.

"He's obviously one of the best," Dunham says of Brodeur. "I learned by watching Marty all the time. You certainly can learn a lot just by watching."

When the call came in June 1998 that he'd been the Predators' first pick in the expansion draft, Dunham was thrilled. So, too, were the fans, 15,500 of whom turn out on average to every home game.

"He's been great," says Predators' head coach Barry Trotz. "Hopefully we can reduce the shots on him, but Mike's been saying he doesn't mind getting a decent number of shots. It keeps him in the game and it keeps him mentally focused. From that standpoint, he could be the perfect goalie for us."

Turns out someone else agrees, someone Dunham once worked under.

"I'm not surprised at what he's done," says Martin Brodeur. "He just needed to get a chance, so it was just a matter of time."

All hockey players remember their NHL debut, and Mike Dunham is no exception. It was early in the 1996–97 season, and Dunham, who was then tending net for New Jersey, was told he'd be starting in a game at the United Center against Chicago. He did what he'd always done prior to any game: he ate, he napped, he prepared himself. But after the game was over, and after Dunham had helped steer the Devils to a 4-2 victory, the feeling was anything but usual. "I think there was a feeling of satisfaction in myself knowing that I finally got to play and especially that we won," recalls Dunham. "I think I proved to myself that I could play at this level, because you never know if you can until you do it."

Year	Team	Lea	REGULAR SEASON								PLAYOFFS						
			GP	W	L	T	Mins	GA	SO	Avg	GP	W	L	Mins	GA	SO	Avg
1989-90	Canterbury	H.S.	32	....	....	....	1558	68	3	1.96	....	....	....	....	....	....	....
1990-91	Uni of Maine	H.E.	23	14	5	2	1275	63	0	2.96	....	....	....	....	....	....	....
	United States	WJC-A	3	....	....	....	180	11	....	3.67	....	....	....	....	....	....	....
1991-92	Uni of Maine	H.E.	7	6	0	0	382	14	1	2.20	....	....	....	....	....	....	....
	United States	WJC-A	6	5	0	1	360	14	....	2.33	....	....	....	....	....	....	....
	United States	Nat-Team	3	0	1	1	157	10	0	3.82	....	....	....	....	....	....	....
	United States	Olympics	DID NOT PLAY - SPARE GOALTENDER														
	United States	WC-A	3	0	1	0	107	7	....	3.92	....	....	....	....	....	....	....
1992-93	Univ. Maine	H.E.	25	21	1	1	1429	63	0	2.65	....	....	....	....	....	....	....
	United States	WC-A	1	1	0	0	60	1	0	1.00	....	....	....	....	....	....	....
1993-94	United States	Nat-Team	33	22	9	2	1983	125	2	3.78	....	....	....	....	....	....	....
	U.S. Olympic		3	0	1	2	180	15	0	5.00	....	....	....	....	....	....	....
	Albany	AHL	5	2	2	1	304	26	0	5.12	....	....	....	....	....	....	....
1994-95	Albany	AHL	35	20	7	8	2120	99	1	2.80	7	6	1	419	20	1	2.86
1995-96	Albany	AHL	44	30	10	2	2592	109	1	2.52	3	1	2	182	5	1	1.65
1996-97	New Jersey	NHL	26	8	7	1	1013	43	2	2.55	....	....	....	....	....	....	....
	Albany	AHL	3	1	1	1	184	12	0	3.91	....	....	....	....	....	....	....
1997-98	New Jersey	NHL	15	5	5	3	773	29	1	2.25	....	....	....	....	....	....	....
	United States	WC-A	2	0	1	0	40	4	0	6.00	....	....	....	....	....	....	....
1998-99	Nashville	NHL	44	16	23	3	2472	127	1	3.08	....	....	....	....	....	....	....

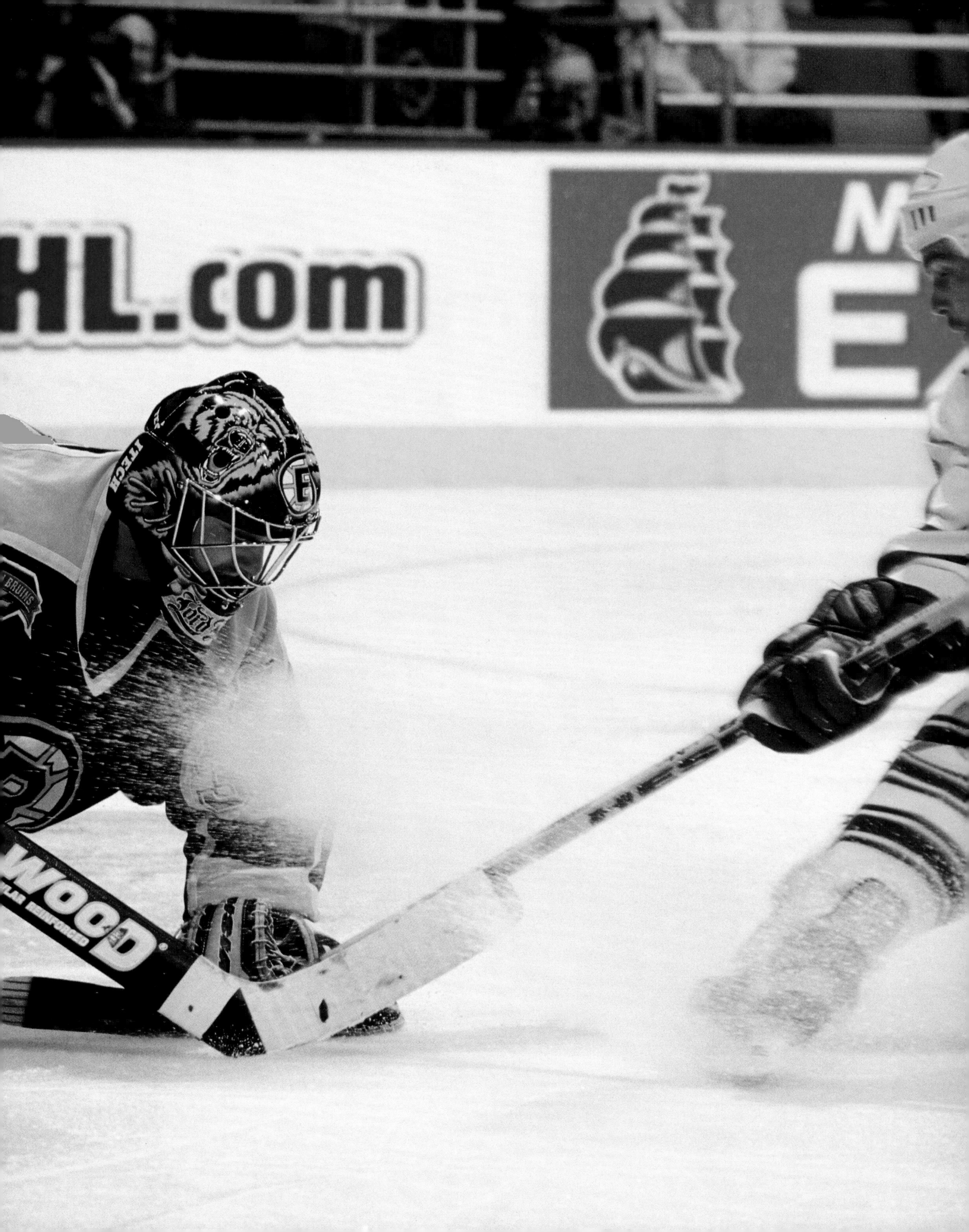
HL.com
ITECH
WOOD
REINFORCED

Masks

It was January 7, 1930.

A 33-year-old goalie by the name of Clint Benedict was in net for the Montreal Maroons. The Maroons were facing the Montreal Canadiens that night, and superstar Howie Morenz was suited up for the opposition, determined as always to help his team pull off a win.

Morenz did get a shot that game, a rocket, in fact. He blasted it squarely in Benedict's direction, and it struck the goaltender between the eyes, slicing open his forehead and shattering his nose and cheekbones.

Few would have known it at the time, but hockey was about to change forever.

1959

Benedict was taken away for repairs, as goalies often were in the those days. But when he returned, some six weeks later, on February 20, he brought along a piece of apparatus that no one had ever seen before. A mask.

By all accounts, it was a crude contraption. It was made of leather and wire and left only his eyes exposed. Benedict might have felt a little more protected, but he wasn't thrilled with the mask's design. "The nosepiece protruded too far and obscured my vision on low shots," he later recalled.

Funny how times have changed. Today's guardians would no sooner leave off the mask than hit the ice without their pads and skates.

The mask—at least, that particular mask—wasn't destined to last for long. The Maroons lost 2-0 to Chicago the night Benedict returned from his injuries, and the goaltender felt the new piece of equipment was the reason why. He promptly threw it away, after wearing it only once.

Funny how times have changed. Today's guardians would no sooner leave off the mask than hit the ice without their pads and skates. But at one time, not really so long ago, it was customary for all goaltenders to head into battle barefaced.

The great Georges Vezina never wore a mask, nor did any of his immediate successors, John Roach, Roy Worters, George Hainsworth or Cecil "Tiny" Thompson. In fact, it wasn't until November 1, 1959—almost three decades after Clint Benedict first appeared on the ice with a leather faceguard attached to his head—that attitudes toward face protection began to change for good.

That night, Jacques Plante and his Montreal Canadiens were visitors at New York's Madison Square Garden. Plante, a solitary netminder who preferred to stay in his hotel room and knit hats and sweaters on road trips than hit the town with his teammates, had long been lobbying to wear a facemask during games. However, Canadiens coach Toe Blake had objected, arguing that a mask would reduce his goaltender's field of vision.

But Plante was not the kind of guy who'd easily abandon an idea he believed in. After suffering numerous facial injuries, including two broken cheekbones, four broken noses and a fractured skull, Plante teamed up with a Montreal businessman and had a plastic mask designed. He dared only to use it in practice—until that night in New York.

Andy Bathgate took a backhander, and Plante immediately fell to the ice, blood gushing from his wound. He left the ice and the game was delayed while doctors sewed seven stitches to close the cut.

Plante confronted his coach and delivered an ultimatum. "I won't go back in without the mask," he's reported to have said. Blake complied with the demand, Plante returned to the game, and the mask did anything but inhibit his performance. The Canadiens won 3-1 that night, as they compiled an 18-game unbeaten streak.

Plante, who would finish his career with a record seven Vezina Trophy's in his trophy case, not only continued to wear a goalie mask, but also became greatly involved in the design of the masks worn by most of the professional goalies of his time.

One by one, the guardians began to shield their faces. Terry Sawchuk wore his a few years after Plante. Later, Glenn Hall did the same, as did Johnny Bower, who'd taken more than 200 stitches to his face during most of his goaltending career. Eventually, even Gump Worsley, who'd complained that the mask made his face hot and prevented him from seeing properly, joined the crowd, but not until his final season. "Anyone who wears one is chicken," he'd long argued. "My face is my mask."

By 1975, the maskless netminder became a thing of the past, and the style of goaltending began to change as much as the look of the goaltender. The fear factor was considerably reduced, and goalies began to use their bodies to protect the net. They became less inclined to do the things their predecessors did—to stay upright and rely on their pads to defend the goal—and more apt to jump headfirst into the middle of play, if that's what it took to stop the puck.

But even though the mask became standard

1961

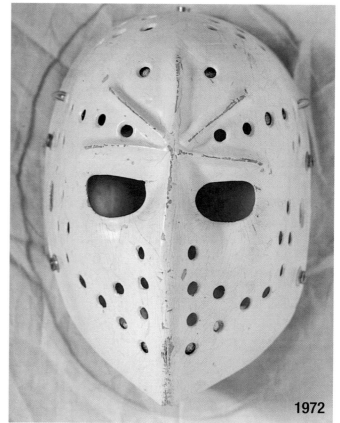

1972

75

equipment for a goalie, its design was constantly fluctuating. Even the masks worn as recently as the 1970s, the kind worn by goalies like Ken Dryden that covered the face but not the back of the head, seem primitive by today's standards.

Today's goalie masks are lightweight, usually between two and two-and-a-half pounds, and are designed to protect every part of the head, as well as the throat. They're constructed from materials like titanium and are built not only to save the goalie, but also to help the goalie make the save. The mask, in other words, has become yet another means of deflecting that nasty chunk of rubber.

Still, when it comes to headwear, safety and save-making are just two of a netminder's concerns. Comfort is also high on the priority list. The mask should be free of pressure points and have a fit that's just right: snug but not too snug.

But Greg Goyer, a former college- and junior-level goalie from Quebec who's now production manager for the goalie equipment manufactured by Itech, says in his experience, there's something else besides comfort and protection that most goalies value in a mask.

"Goalies are really conscious of the look," Goyer says. "They really are a different breed of player."

The demand, he says, is for a specific style, something that's not too bulky, that has sleek lines and an aerodynamic look. In most cases, goalies also want their headgear personalized. In other words, custom painted.

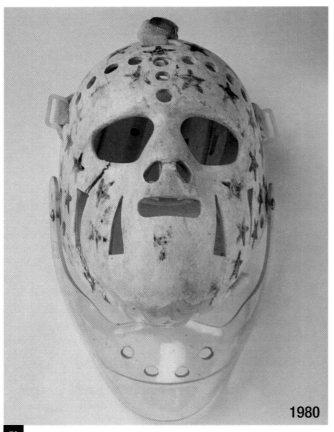

1980

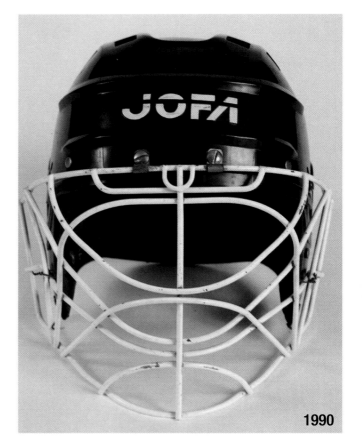

1990

It was in the early 1970s, says Goyer, that goalies first began to have their masks painted, primarily because they wanted to exude a sense of individuality.

In the case of Gerry Cheevers, who led the Boston Bruins to Stanley Cup wins in 1970 and 1972, the search for identity resulted in a mask that was covered with stitches, in precisely the places where he was hit by the puck. By the time he retired, there were few empty spaces remaining, and the masks—he got a new one every year—had become legendary. One even made its way into a museum in Sweden.

There may be no NHL masks decorated with stitches around today, but Cheevers' idea—to design a mask that made him look tough and intimidating—has certainly persisted. Goyer says it boils down to this: the more menacing the mask, the better the goalie is thought to be.

"Goalies don't want anything that's per-

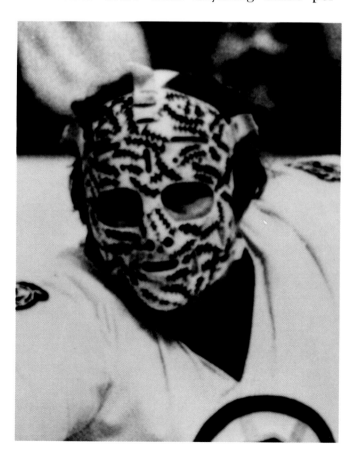

Longest undefeated streak
by a goaltender from start of career:
Patrick Lalime - 16

Most 40-or-more win seasons
by a goaltender:
Jacques Plante - 3

Most consecutive 40-or-more win
seasons by a goaltender:
Terry Sawchuk - 2

Most 30-or-more win seasons
by a goaltender:
Patrick Roy - 8

Most consecutive 30-or-more win
seasons by a goaltender:
Tony Esposito - 7

Most losses by a goaltender, career:
Gump Worsley - 352

Most losses by a goaltender,
one season:
Gary Smith - 48

ceived as childish," he says.

In Olaf Kolzig's case, there's nothing remotely childish about the artwork on his head. Kolzig's mask is decorated with a picture of a gorilla, and the word "Zilla"—just one of the Washington netminder's nicknames—is written at the bottom.

Patrick Roy's mask bears the image of a menacing avalanche, and Curtis Joseph's is painted with a picture of a vicious, wolflike beast, jaws sprung and ready to attack.

But they're not all designed to elicit terror. As Goyer says, there's something else at play in goalie mask design: a quest to establish a little personal identity. Ron Tugnutt and Jeff Hackett are just two goalies who've imprinted the back of their masks with the names of their kids. Joseph's has a picture of a four-leaf clover that bears the initials of his wife and three children.

In Byron Dafoe's case, it's not kids, but animals. His dogs, Vamp and Zona, have their names on his headgear.

Ed Belfour has the menacing part down pat—his trademark eagle is painted on his goalie mask—but his mask also has a gentler piece of artwork: the logo for the Make-a-Wish Foundation, which Belfour has long supported.

There have been masks with images of mad dogs, of lightning, of snakes—even of beer. Ottawa's Tugnutt had his mask painted with a picture of the amber ale, an idea he came up with after being traded from Anaheim to Montreal.

"Since the Canadiens belong to Molson [a Canadian brewery], I wondered how throwing a

> Ed Belfour has the menacing part down pat—his trademark eagle is painted on his goalie mask—but his mask also has a gentler piece of artwork: the logo for the Make-a-Wish Foundation, which Belfour has long supported.

jug of Molson Ice beer would look on my mask," says Tugnutt. The result is Tugnutt's signature Splash design, which he decided to take with him when he made the move to Ottawa.

In many ways, the goalie mask has become a piece of equipment that's not only used to protect and individualize, but which can also be regarded as a work of art. Gump Worsley would probably be mighty confused, and no doubt a little disdainful, if he could see the arty helmet on Curtis Joseph's head, but other former netminders would certainly applaud the fact that all NHL netminders now wear goalie masks, whether they're painted with wild creatures or not.

Gary Smith, who played with eight different NHL teams in the space of 14 years, is one such goalie. He long resisted the idea of putting on a facemask, in spite of the fact that he was terrified of being hit by the puck. One day he stopped resisting. It was the day his fellow netminder was hit by a shot in the throat.

"I was on the bench and I knew I'd be going in," he says. "I didn't have my mask with me, but I turned to the equipment manager and said, 'Go get my mask.' I never played without one again."

Itech's Goyer says attitudes toward equipment—specifically the mask—definitely distinguish hockey's contemporary goaltenders from their predecessors. "I hear a lot of goaltenders say that when they look back at the time when goalies didn't wear masks, they never would have played," he says.

Today, thank goodness, they do play—and they play like they've never played before. Gone are the days when a goaltender had to worry as much about breaking a nose as stopping a puck. Gone are the days when games were routinely interrupted to allow a doctor to stitch up a netminder's forehead.

In many ways, points out Goyer, something else is also gone. The longstanding stereotype of the goaltender-as-oddball, perpetuated in large measure by the man who tended nets barefaced, has also been eroded.

Today, hockey's guardians are suitably dressed for battle when they stand before the crease. Yes, they look unique. Yes, they look intimidating.

And yes, they look considerably different than their forefathers. The change was slow in coming, but it has done wonders for the men behind the mask.

Patrick Roy

33 COLORADO AVALANCHE

When they think of Patrick Roy, most hockey fans think of the playoffs. Because the post-season is where Roy's star has shone the brightest in a dazzling 14-year career.

And so it should come as no surprise, then, that when you ask the Colorado Avalanche goaltender to pick out one virtuoso performance among so many brilliant symphonies, he'll take you back to a playoff game his first year in the league.

Roy, then playing for the Montreal Canadiens, was facing the New York Rangers in the eastern conference finals. The winner would be heading to the Stanley Cup, the loser to the golf course.

The Canadiens won the first two games in Montreal over the favored Blue Shirts. Before Game 3 back at Madison Square Garden, Ranger forward Wilf Paiement questioned Roy's performance in the first two games.

"Anyone can make 20 saves. Let's see what he can do with 40 shots."

As dumb things to say go, challenging Roy before a game had to be one of the dumbest. The Rangers bombarded Roy with 47 shots in that game, which ended tied after regulation.

"I felt they could not score on me," Roy would remember of the overtime. "It was the kind of feeling you maybe get two or three times in your career. And I had it at the right moment.

"I can't recall the exact players but I can remember the sequence of the plays from the game. I can remember someone coming out on the angle, passing across, I make the save with my blocker, the puck bounces in the air and it goes to the blue line, a guy takes a shot, I make the save, rebound, save.

"If I had to pick out one performance that was my greatest, I think that would have to be it. For now, at least."

Yes, for now. Because who knows how many more great performances Patrick Roy has in him.

When the history of goaltending in the National Hockey League during this century is written, the name Patrick Roy will find a spot among a small group of netminders who were clearly in a league of their own. Goaltenders who in some ways changed the game, goaltenders whose performances raised the standard by which all of hockey's backstoppers would be judged.

Early in his career, Roy would influence a generation of young goaltenders in his home province of Quebec. And to no one's surprise, it wouldn't be long after his arrival that the National Hockey League would see a string of backstoppers entering the league whose game was modelled on the kid from the Quebec City suburb of Ste. Foy who is known as St. Patrick.

While Roy's butterfly style, honed by the great goaltending coach, Francois Allaire, has been credited for much of his success, it is something that goaltending coaches can't teach that has made Patrick Roy the great goaltender that he is.

A will to win.

"In my 20 years in this game, I've seen some great players and some great people," says Avalanche GM Pierre Lacroix. "But I have never seen anyone with Patrick Roy's drive to win. I have never seen anyone who hated to lose as much as Patrick Roy.

"That's something you can't invent or create. That's something that's inside you and it's always been inside Patrick."

Like his passion for victory, Patrick Roy's love for the position he plays has always been inside him.

He remembers the first day he went to the arena with his mother and older brother to sign up for hockey.

"I said to my mother, 'I want to be a goaltender.' So my mother says to the person, 'I have two boys who want to play hockey but Patrick absolutely wants to be a goaltender.' "

They let him be a goaltender.

It was really no surprise to the Roy family. Young Patrick loved playing road hockey with his friends. Because he was the smallest, he always played goal. On Saturday evenings, he would watch "Hockey Night in Canada." He would play hockey inside the house, strapping pillows to his legs for goalie pads.

One of Roy's early heroes was Daniel Bouchard, a top Quebec goalie who would also play in the NHL for the Calgary Flames among other teams. One of the most cherished items of Roy's youth was a goalie stick given to him by Bouchard. It meant so much to him that he even began sleeping with the stick in hopes that if he held on to it tight enough, his dream of making it to the NHL one day might come true.

He must have squeezed it pretty tight.

Roy developed into a top amateur goalie and was soon being scouted by some of the top teams in the Quebec junior league. After Grade 10, Roy decided not to attend Grade 11 and instead go to the training camp of the Granby Bisons.

He would make the team, spending three seasons with the club and facing more rubber than a highway. But the 40 and 50 shots a game that Roy faced with the defensively-inept Bisons helped make him a better goalie. In the summer of 1984, the Montreal Canadiens used their fourth-round selection in the NHL entry draft to pick Roy.

A star was born.

Roy would make the big club in 1985–86, at the age of 20, unusually young for the position he played. And it wasn't long before the hockey world would be introduced to some of his quirky habits. Like talking to his goal posts.

"I talk to my goal posts. They're my friends. They listen," Roy said. "It's a superstition." Just like his penchant for not skating across the red line or blue lines on the ice on his way to and from his goal.

Roy also likes to stand between the blue line and his net for the national anthem that precedes every game. After the anthem is finished, Roy stares at his net intently for several seconds before skating as fast as he can towards it and then doing a couple of figure eights before getting in final position to start the game.

Roy also puts his equipment on in the same order before every game. Eccentric? No. Just another superstition.

"They're there for one purpose for me," Roy says. "They make me feel comfortable. They make me confident at the same time and help me to concentrate."

Unlike many goalies who are usually quiet in the dressing room before and during games, Patrick Roy has become known for being the opposite. During particularly tough games, playoff games that have gone into overtime, for instance, it is often Roy who will stand up and inspire his teammates with a pep talk.

Many times Roy has told his fellow players when the game has gone into extra minutes: "You worry about scoring the goal. They will not score on me, I promise you." And more often than not, Roy has upheld his end of the bargain.

During one remarkable streak during the 1993 playoffs, Roy and the Montreal Canadiens won 10 games in overtime. The Habs would win the Cup that year and Roy the Conn Smythe Trophy, as most valuable player in the post-season.

Roy had won the Conn Smythe in 1986 as well. And while he didn't win playoff MVP in his third Cup win with the Colorado Avalanche in 1996, Roy easily could have.

Roy, of course, was traded to Colorado earlier that season after a much-publicized dust-up with then Montreal coach Mario Tremblay. Tensions

> **Many times Roy has told his fellow players when the game has gone into extra minutes: "You worry about scoring the goal. They will not score on me, I promise you."**

between the goalie and his coach came to a head on December 2, 1995, after Montreal lost in an 11-1 blowout against Detroit. Roy was finally yanked after the ninth Detroit goal. He was furious that he had been left in for so long and figured it was an intentional move by Tremblay to humiliate him.

Roy and Tremblay exchanged some angry words and then Roy got up from his seat on the bench, walked over to team president Ronald Corey, who sat right behind the players, and told him that was the last game he would ever play in a Montreal uniform.

And it was.

While the 1998–99 season may not have been Patrick Roy's greatest statistically, it might have been one of his most satisfying. Roy's year got off to a rocky start. Once seemingly invincible, all of a sudden Roy looked completely vulnerable. Shots from 60 feet away that at one time he would have angled harmlessly to the corner, were going through his legs. And all of a sudden, people were starting to wonder if a 33-year-old who had been in the league 14 years, was finished.

"It was a challenging time, no question," Roy said.

His confidence was shaken. He wondered whether he still possessed any of his old magic. But he hung in there.

"I just kept telling myself I have to go back to the basics," Roy remembered. "I had to start making one save at a time and build off of each save. I had to keep telling myself I could get back to where I was if I stuck to it."

The inner voice that kept telling Roy not to give up knew something. Roy bounced back in the second half of the year, and would finish the year posting a GAA of 2.29. He would also get 32 wins, giving him 381 for his career. Just that much closer to one of the records he would love to break the most—career wins. The record of 447 is held by legendary goalie, Terry Sawchuk.

"That's one of my goals," says Roy. "To pass Sawchuk."

While he would have to wait another year to get a chance at Sawchuk's record, Roy would get the chance this past season to go for another run to the Stanley Cup finals.

And Patrick Roy would show the world that he hadn't lost any of his old magic. It simply went missing for awhile.

When it comes to commitment, nothing stands between Patrick Roy and the game he adores—not even appendicitis. In 1994, when Roy was tending nets for the Montreal Canadiens, he was hit with an appendicitis attack during the first round of the playoffs. Turns out it takes a lot more than that to keep this goalie down. Roy missed the third game of the series against Boston, but convinced doctors to postpone surgery and let him return for the fourth. Roy was given antibiotics, left the hospital, and ended up stopping 39 shots that night to lead the Canadiens to a 5-2 victory. "I couldn't even put my pants on," Roy said later, recalling the pain. "It's not something I recommend to anybody."

			REGULAR SEASON								PLAYOFFS						
Year	Team	Lea	GP	W	L	T	Mins	GA	SO	Avg	GP	W	L	Mins	GA	SO	Avg
1982-83	Granby	QMJHL	54	13	35	1	2808	293	0	6.26	....	....	....	....	....	....	....
1983-84	Granby	QMJHL	61	29	29	1	3585	265	0	4.44	4	0	4	244	22	0	5.41
1984-85	Montreal	NHL	1	1	0	0	20	0	0	0.00	....	....	....	....	....	....	....
	Granby	QMJHL	44	16	25	1	2463	228	0	5.55	....	....	....	....	....	....	....
	Sherbrooke	AHL	1	1	0	0	60	4	0	4.00	13	10	3	769	37	0	2.89
1985-86	Montreal	NHL	47	23	18	3	2651	148	1	3.35	20	15	5	1218	39	1	1.92
1986-87	Montreal	NHL	46	22	16	6	2686	131	1	2.93	6	4	2	330	22	0	4.00
1987-88	Montreal	NHL	45	23	12	9	2586	125	3	2.90	8	3	4	430	24	0	3.35
1988-89	Montreal	NHL	48	33	5	6	2744	113	4	2.47	19	13	6	1206	42	2	2.09
1990-91	Montreal	NHL	48	25	15	6	2835	128	1	2.71	13	7	5	785	40	0	3.06
1991-92	Montreal	NHL	67	36	22	8	3935	155	5	2.36	11	4	7	686	30	1	2.62
1992-93	Montreal	NHL	62	31	25	5	3595	192	2	3.20	20	16	4	1293	46	0	2.13
1993-94	Montreal	NHL	68	35	17	11	3867	161	7	2.50	6	3	3	375	16	0	2.56
1994-95	Montreal	NHL	43	17	20	6	2566	127	1	2.97	....	....	....	....	....	....	....
1995-96	Montreal	NHL	22	12	9	1	1260	62	1	2.95	....	....	....	....	....	....	....
	Colorado	NHL	39	22	15	1	2305	103	1	2.68	22	16	6	1454	51	3	2.10
1996-97	Colorado	NHL	62	38	15	7	3698	143	7	2.32	17	10	7	1034	38	3	2.21
1997-98	Colorado	NHL	65	31	19	13	3835	153	4	2.39	7	3	4	430	18	0	2.51
	Canada	Olympics	6	3	3	0	369	9	1	1.46	....	....	....	....	....	....	....
1998-99	Colorado	NHL	61	32	19	8	3648	139	5	2.29	19	11	8	1173	52	1	2.66

Mike Richter

35 NEW YORK RANGERS

New Yorkers love their Broadway, their Times Square and their Statue of Liberty. But they also love something else: their No. 1 Rangers goalie.

Mike Richter may have hailed from elsewhere—he was born in Abington, Pennsylvania 33 years ago—but he's become as much a part of the New York landscape as the Empire State Building. After all, he's been guarding the nets in the Big Apple for 10 happy years. The fans consider him family, and the feeling, apparently, is mutual.

"I always felt that if I had the choice, I'd make a smart choice to stay where I'm happy and where I feel my allegiance is," says Richter. "And that place is New York."

Richter first became part of the Rangers' organization in 1985 when he was the second-round pick in the entry draft. He didn't make an immediate move to New York, however, instead playing two seasons with the University of Wisconsin, where he went 14-9-0 in his

first year and 19-16-1 in his second.

The following season, Richter made his professional goaltending debut. On March 1, 1988, just a few days after playing with the U.S. Olympic team, he donned a Colorado Rangers jersey in the IHL and led the team to a 3-1 victory over

Kalamazoo. During the next month, he posted a 13-3-0 record and helped Colorado win the West Division title.

It wouldn't be the last time he posted astounding stats. During his 1988–89 campaign with Denver, Richter led all IHL goalies in games played, with 57, and ranked second in minutes, with 3,301.

And he hadn't yet played in the big leagues. Richter's regular-season NHL debut would take place on October 19, 1989. No. 35 would lead the Rangers to a 7-3 decision over the Hartford Whalers at Madison Square Garden, and the love-in with Ranger fans would begin.

It's never really abated—and neither has the record-setting. Richter, who stands five-foot-eleven and weighs 185 pounds, has been named a finalist for the Vezina Trophy, an NHL All-Star Game MVP and a member of the All-Time

He holds Rangers' records for most wins in a season, most saves in a game, most career playoff shutouts and highest save percentage in a regular season.

USA Hockey Team. He holds Rangers' records for most wins in a season, most saves in a game, most career playoff shutouts and highest save percentage in the regular season.

Then, too, there was that one season, back in 1993–94, when Richter went 42-12-6 in the regular season and 16-7 in the playoffs to lead the Rangers into possession of that most coveted chunk of metal, the Stanley Cup.

Ask former teammate Wayne Gretzky what he thinks of Richter, and the praise is effusive.

"He's a world-class goaltender and he's extremely well-liked," says Gretzky. "He's on his game right now, he's played extraordinarily."

Ask television analyst and former goaltender John Davidson his opinion, and you'll also hear accolades.

"If people had a chance to know him, to understand his preparation and his commitment to being the best he can be, it's quite remarkable," says Davidson.

Ask the fans what they think of their backstopper, a goalie who's known for being superbly conditioned, mentally sharp and who possesses a stellar work ethic, and they may end up gushing about a particular save Richter made.

Ask the fans what they think of their backstopper, a goalie who's known for being superbly conditioned, mentally sharp and who possesses a stellar work ethic, and they may end up gushing about a particular save Richter made. Like the one, for instance, back on October 16, 1998 when the Rangers faced the New York Islanders.

That was the night when the Islanders' Claude Lapointe was handed a penalty shot late in the third period. The Rangers were up 3-2.

When the whistle blew, Lapointe took off down the ice. Richter moved away from his cage, forcing Lapointe to deke, then backskated as quickly as Lapointe was moving, and thrust out his pad to repel a backhand shot. The record-keepers would note that Richter had saved nine of the 10 penalty shots he'd faced in his career.

"On penalty shots against Mike, if they score, I'm surprised," Rangers' captain Brian Leetch would later observe. "Certainly, I've played against him enough in practice to know that if he's facing a breakaway and he has time to get set, he skates so well and he's so quick that he's almost always going to stop you."

Fast, yes. Focused, certainly. But off the ice, Mike Richter is equally impressive.

This, after all, is a guy who's worked tirelessly

for charity—primarily for the kids of New York City.

He's won the Thurman Munson Award for his charity work and the Sloan Kettering Award of Courage for his hospital work. In 1996, he raised $2,000 for pediatric patients at the New York Hospital-Cornell Medical Center by auctioning off the Harley-Davidson he won for being MVP of the World Cup of Hockey.

World-class guy, world-class goaltender.

"Mike Richter is one of the elite goaltenders in this league and he's at the top of his game," says his coach, John Muckler.

Funny, though: in spite of the accomplishments, in spite of the praise, Mike Richter still feels there's room for improvement.

"I'm not where I want to be yet," he says, "but I'm getting there."

New Yorkers, no doubt, will be watching expectantly.

Summertime, for many NHL players, translates into a time to kick back and hit the beach or the golf course. Not so for Mike Richter. Instead, summer has become the time when he's headed for school, to work on completing the college degree he put on hold in 1987 when he left the University of Wisconsin. As Richter sees it, it's an investment in the future, the years ahead when he won't be guarding a hockey net. Richter has been taking courses, one credit at a time, and has been studying such things as economics, history and philosophy. And yes, he's discovered that goalies like students have much in common. "You don't just, one day, cram for an exam, just like you don't, all of a sudden, just show up for the playoffs. It's one of those things where, if you're doing your homework, applying yourself in a big way and learning from your mistakes, you will improve and play great."

					REGULAR SEASON								PLAYOFFS				
Year	Team	Lea	GP	W	L	T	Mins	GA	SO	Avg	GP	W	L	Mins	GA	SO	Avg
1988-89	Denver	IHL	57	23	26	0	3031	217	1	4.30	4	0	4	210	21	0	6.00
	N.Y. Rangers	NHL	....	....	....	....	....	....	....	....	1	0	1	58	4	0	4.14
1989-90	N.Y. Rangers	NHL	23	12	5	5	1320	66	0	3.00	6	3	2	330	19	0	3.45
	Flint Spirits	IHL	13	7	4	2	782	49	0	3.76	....	....	....	....	....		....
1990-91	N.Y. Rangers	NHL	45	21	13	7	2596	135	0	3.12	6	2	4	313	14	1	2.68
1991-92	United States	C Cup	7	4	3	0	420	22	....	3.00	....	....	....	....	....		....
	N.Y. Rangers	NHL	41	23	12	2	2298	119	3	3.11	7	4	2	412	24	1	3.50
1992-93	N.Y. Rangers	NHL	38	13	19	3	2105	134	1	3.82	....	....	....	....	....		....
	Binghamton	AHL	5	4	0	1	305	6	0	1.18	....	....	....	....	....		....
	United States	WC-A	4	1	1	2	237	13	....	3.29	....	....	....	....	....		....
1993-94	N.Y. Rangers	NHL	68	42	12	6	3710	159	5	2.57	23	16	7	1417	49	4	2.07
1994-95	N.Y. Rangers	NHL	35	14	17	2	1993	97	2	2.92	7	2	5	384	23	0	3.59
1995-96	N.Y Rangers	NHL	41	24	13	3	2396	107	3	2.68	11	5	6	661	36	0	3.27
1996-97	United States	W Cup	6	4	2	0	370	15	....	2.00	....	....	....	....	....		....
	N.Y. Rangers	NHL	61	33	22	6	3598	161	4	2.68	15	9	6	939	33	3	2.11
1997-98	N.Y. Rangers	NHL	72	21	31	15	4143	184	0	2.66	....	....	....	....	....		....
	United States	Olympics	4	1	3	0	237	14	0	3.55	....	....	....	....	....		....
1998-99	N.Y. Rangers	NHL	68	27	30	8	3878	170	4	2.63	....	....	....	....	....		....

Steve Shields

As Steve Shields well knows, tending goal in Buffalo is a job with its pros and cons.

The downside, of course, is that you tend to sit a lot. That's just an occupational hazard when you happen to be playing backup to a five-time Vezina Trophy winner and a guy who's widely regarded as the best goaltender on the planet.

On the other hand, you can learn a considerable amount when you're perched on the bench and able to watch—and really study—Dominik Hasek's every move.

"I learned a lot about competitiveness, how he fights for the puck and competes to see the puck," says Shields. "The biggest lesson was, if you stay in the right position, you're always going to have a chance to stop the puck."

The education was outstanding, no question about it. But last season, after two years of playing understudy to the Dominator, Shields was given a chance to skate away from the bench and guard a net of his own—clear across the country in an arena they call the Shark Tank.

Shields says he was thrilled when he learned, back in June of 1998, that he'd be heading to San Jose, in spite of the fact that he was once again joining a club with a veteran netminder—in this case, two-time Stanley Cup winner Mike Vernon.

93

"I was really excited about coming to San Jose," recalls Shields. "I look at it as the best of both worlds. Mike Vernon is a proven winner, and he has a lot to offer me personally. Plus, I look at this as a chance to gain some more playing time and experience."

In fact, the 27-year-old Shields, who's a full ten years younger than Vernon, has played plenty. He tended net in 37 games for the Sharks last season, winning 15 of them, and wound up with a save percentage of .921 and a goals-against average of 2.22.

"His greatest strength is his ability to compete," observes Sharks head coach Darryl Sutter. "He is a big goaltender who takes up a lot of room and always seems to be in the right position to make a save."

At six-foot-three and 210 pounds, Shields is certainly no lightweight.

"He really covers a lot of the net," says the Flyers' Eric Lindros. Indeed, Shields' enormous wingspan works to his advantage most nights, not to mention his natural athleticism and powerful competitive instinct.

"Or, as Wayne Thomas, the Sharks' assistant general manager, says: "He's got all the tools."

Of course, anyone who's known Shields for

> **At six-foot-three and 210 pounds, Shields is certainly no lightweight.**

any length of time knows he didn't just acquire those tools yesterday.

The Toronto, Ontario native, who first tended net at the age of seven when his team's regular goaltender was out of town, has been turning heads for a very long time.

From 1990 to 1994, Shields was a standout goalie for the University of Michigan Wolverines, setting an NCAA record for most wins by a goaltender, with 111. Shields was twice named

He's stepped out of the Dominator's shadow and into his own crease.

Central Collegiate Hockey Association First Team All-Star, and in 1994 was a finalist for the Hobey Baker Award, as college hockey MVP.

In 1995–96, the winning pace continued. Shields led the Rochester Americans, Buffalo's top development affiliate, to the AHL's Calder Cup championship. He recorded 15 playoff vic-

tories, the most ever by a goalie in that league.

Shields played just two games for the Sabres that season, but the next year, during the playoffs, he finally had a chance to showcase his ability in the NHL curcible.

Shields stepped in when Hasek was sidelined with injuries in late 1997, and played 10 of the Sabres' 12 playoff games, leading Buffalo into the second round and posting his first-ever career shutout in a match against Ottawa.

"It demonstrated to a lot of people that I could play at this level and make a difference, compete in big games and win," recalls Shields. "I started to build a bit of a name for myself and a bit of respect around the league."

These days, Shields is continuing to earn that respect. He's stepped out of the Dominator's shadow and into his own crease. And inside the Shark Tank, where 17,483 fans roar their approval whenever the Sharks hit the ice, Shields has proved he can live up to his name.

"We have been very pleased," says Thomas. "He has given us a chance to win in every game he has played."

You don't play backup to stellar goalie Dominik Hasek without learning a thing or two—and no one knows that better than Steve Shields. Shields says he learned plenty during his two years in Buffalo, about competitiveness, about drive, about focus. He studied Hasek's positioning and learned to copy the way he drops his stick and covers the puck with two hands. But Shields says Hasek learned something from him, too, something that's a much more . . . private matter. "He mentioned something the other day about that," Shields said not long ago. "He said that from me, he learned how to wear two cups."

			REGULAR SEASON								PLAYOFFS						
Year	Team	Lea	GP	W	L	T	Mins	GA	SO	Avg	GP	W	L	Mins	GA	SO	Avg
1990-91	Univ. Mich.	CCHA	37	26	6	3	1963	106	0	3.24	....	....	....	....	....	....	....
1991-92	Univ. Mich.	CCHA	37	27	7	2	2090	99	1	2.84	....	....	....	....	....	....	....
1992-93	Univ. Mich.	CCHA	39	30	6	2	2027	75	2	2.22	....	....	....	....	....	....	....
1993-94	Univ. Mich.	CCHA	36	28	6	1	1961	87	0	2.66	....	....	....	....	....	....	....
1994-95	Rochester	AHL	13	3	8	0	673	53	0	4.72	1	0	0	20	3	0	9.00
	South Carolina	ECHL	21	11	5	2	1158	52	2	2.69	3	0	2	144	11	0	4.58
1995-96	Buffalo	NHL	2	1	0	0	75	4	0	3.20	....	....	....	....	....	....	....
	Rochester	AHL	43	20	17	2	2357	140	1	3.56	19	15	3	1127	47	1	2.50
1996-97	Buffalo	NHL	13	3	8	2	789	39	0	2.97	10	4	6	570	26	1	2.74
	Rochester	AHL	23	14	6	2	1331	60	1	2.70	....	....	....	....	....	....	....
1997-98	Buffalo	NHL	16	3	6	4	785	37	0	2.83	....	....	....	....	....	....	....
	Rochester	AHL	1	0	1	0	59	3	0	3.04	....	....	....	....	....	....	....
1998-99	San Jose	NHL	37	15	11	8	2162	80	4	2.22	1	0	1	60	6	0	6.00

Equipment

Equipment.

Equipment.

Equipment.

Ask any NHL goalie past or present what has been the single biggest change in their position over the past several decades and you're liable to get the same answer.

The equipment.

The catching gloves are bigger, the leg pads are lighter, and, of course, the modern-day goalie masks have all but eliminated the netminder's greatest fear—injury to the face.

And better protection has had a dramatic impact on the way goaltenders now play the position.

Where once upon a time goaltenders were reluctant to go down for fear of a shot to the face or upper body, today's goalies have no such qualms. And as this hockey

century comes to a close, the stand-up goalie of yesterday has become all but extinct.

Changes in equipment have offered goaltenders so many perceived advantages, in fact, that the NHL has recently had to crack down on the dimensions of virtually everything a goalie puts on for a game.

And as the NHL continues to look for ways to increase scoring, goaltenders are likely to undergo even further scrutiny into the next century. Goaltenders who played in the NHL before the equipment revolution of the last two decades find themselves more than a little envious.

"I just wish some of the stuff they have now was around when I was playing," says Gary Smith, who played for 14 seasons in the NHL before retiring in 1980.

While the modern mask has had the biggest impact on the position, even goalie skates offer far better protection than they once did.

In fact, Smith remembers putting on sock upon sock during the course of the season, to offer his feet better protection inside his skate from the inevitable pain of a slap-shot off the toe.

One season, he wore 16 pair of socks under his skates. The resulting padding was so thick, he remembers, that "the socks became almost like a cast."

Still, the equipment Smith had access to throughout his career was a far cry from the makeshift protection and padding goaltenders appended to themselves at the beginning of the century.

The first goaltender known to have worn leg pads in Stanley Cup competition was George

> Goaltenders who played in the NHL before the equipment revolution of the last two decades find themselves more than a little envious.

"Whitey" Merritt, who tended the nets for the Winnipeg Victoria team that captured hockey's greatest trophy in 1896. After Merritt appeared in net wearing cricket pads, goaltenders for the next three decades wore pads that closely resembled those worn by cricketers.

The 1920s brought further changes. A Hamilton harness and leather worker named Emil Kenesky, having noticed that many goals were being scored by pucks deflecting off the rounded, cricket-style pads of the goalie, experimented with his own design. Result: Kenesky pads were made of horsehide and tough cotton sheeting, and were 12 inches wide so they extended out from the leg instead of curving around it.

They were an instant hit.

The next big advancement in equipment would come in the 1947–48 season during a game between the Chicago Blackhawks and Detroit Red Wings.

It was during this contest that Blackhawks netminder Emile "The Cat" Francis appeared in goal wearing a baseball glove. Specifically, a first baseman's trapper. Until this time, goalies had been using gloves very similar to those used by forwards and defensemen, with a strip of leather sewn between the thumb and forefinger on the catching hand.

As changes to the equipment worn by goaltenders go, the next dramatic equipment change—the face mask—had the single biggest impact on the position and the way it was played. "It eliminated the fear that came with the position," said former NHL goaltender Glen Hanlon. "And all of a sudden goalies weren't afraid to go down any more."

In the 1970s, another Chicago netminder, Tony Esposito, made waves by customizing his equipment—changes that were responsible for the growth in the size of the catching glove, which became known as "the cheater." Esposito also doctored other pieces of his equipment to help take away space from the shooters.

By the 1980s, the goalie equipment business was booming. And each company was determined to top the other with equipment that was lighter, bigger and gave the goalie a greater advantage.

Within the next decade, goaltenders appeared to have almost doubled in size. Perhaps most dramatic of all were the wide-winged shoulder pads worn by former Philadelphia Flyers goaltender Garth Snow, now with the Vancouver Canucks.

As goaltenders blew up to the size of the Michelin man, scoring consequently dropped

While the size of the equipment perhaps gave shooters less of a target, what the new equipment offered that had an even bigger impact on the position was its high degree of protection.

off, and finally the league stepped in following the 1997–98 season to downsize and regulate equipment worn by goaltenders throughout the league.

While the size of the equipment perhaps gave shooters less of a target, what the new equipment offered that had an even bigger impact on the position was its high degree of protection.

"When I began playing in 1980, there was no way I could take a shot in my chest or upper body or shoulders and not pay the price for it," says NHL goalie Andy Moog, who retired 18 years later after a stellar career. "As a result, in the early

1980s, the upper body and high shots you saved with your hands, quite frankly you didn't save a lot of them. They scored on you up there.

"Today, the equipment is manufactured in such a way [that] you don't need to take your hands from down low to up high, you can use your upper body. You can use your head now if you want to."

While Glenn Hall is credited with introducing the butterfly style that is so prevalent in today's NHL—going down with your legs spread in an inverted "V" formation so your pads cover the ice from post to post—it wasn't until goalies became better protected that the technique gained widespread acceptance. Hardly any goalie wanted to go down to face 100-mph slap shots if there was a chance he was going to be hurt with a puck to his face or shoulders.

Today, those shots might just sting a little.

The equipment changes have also allowed goaltenders to practice more aggressively and for a greater length of time. "Before, the equipment was so heavy you could only do so much in practice before you were worn out," says former NHL goalie Greg Millen. "But now, you can take any kind of shot in practice too. Before, you'd take a shot in the shoulder and you'd be done. Not anymore."

As equipment allowed goaltenders to change the way they played, bigger, stronger and faster players also meant changes for the netminder. Kelly Hrudey, who enjoyed a lengthy NHL career before retiring to the broadcast booth in 1998, said he was forced to change his style a hundred percent over the course of his 15 years in the league.

"When I came in during the early 1980s, I was a stand-up goaltender like all the guys back

Before the 1998–99 season, the NHL introduced several rule changes governing the dimensions of goaltender's equipment. The changes were a response to the ballooning appearance of goaltenders and the corresponding decline in goal scoring throughout the league. The rule changes affected several areas of the equipment. Some of these included:

Chest and arm pads i) No raised ridges are allowed on the front edges or sides of the chest pad, the inside or outside of the arms or across the shoulders; ii) Layering at the elbow is permitted to add protection but not to add stopping area; iii) On each side of the shoulder clavicle, protectors are not to exceed seven inches in width.

Pants The maximum width of the thigh pad across the front of the leg is 11 inches.

Jerseys i) Can only be 30 inches at the bottom; 14 inches at top of the sleeve, nine inches at bottom of sleeve; ii) No "tying down" of the sweater is allowed at the wrists if it creates a tension across the jersey such that a "webbing effect" is created in the armpit area; iii) The length of the jersey is illegal if it covers any area between the goalie's legs.

Catching glove A maximum perimeter of 48 inches is permitted. (This is a rule that was to be introduced for the 1999-2000 season. It was 50 inches for the previous season.)

The NHL also introduced random checks of goaltenders' equipment, with any violations of the rules resulting in an automatic one-game suspension.

1920s

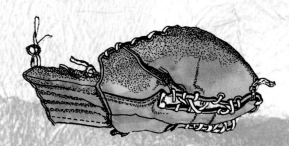

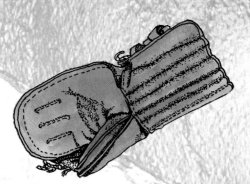

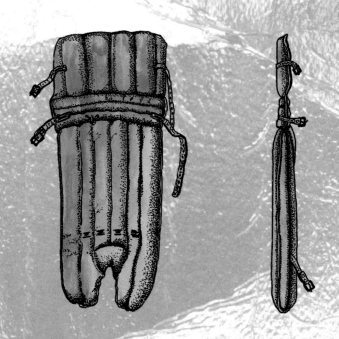

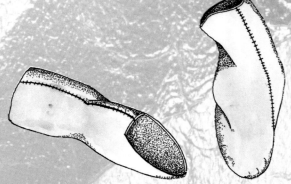

1990s

then, or most of them," Hrudey told an interviewer. "But when we played the Edmonton Oilers we could not stand up and play the angles three feet outside the crease. All those players from Europe would go around you or pass the puck. We had to learn to play deep and still take the five-hole away."

Today's NHL goalie often acts as a third defenseman, using league rules which prohibit players from checking goaltenders when they stray from their crease, to go out and handle the puck at will.

Hrudey wasn't the only goalie during that period who was forced to change—Mike Vernon, Grant Fuhr, Andy Moog, all moved from a stand-up style to the butterfly technique.

Although it was Hall who introduced the butterfly style to the NHL, credit goes to Patrick Roy for refining the technique to the art form it has become today.

Roy, under the direction of goaltending coach Francois Allaire, designed a style that eliminated many of the scoring opportunities down low. Allaire realized that 70 percent of goals in the NHL were scored from a foot or less off the ice. The key was coming up with a style that eliminated more of the area in this prime scoring range.

Roy's enormous success bred a whole generation of Patrick Roy—wannabes in his home province of Quebec. Future NHL goaltenders like Martin Brodeur and Felix Potvin would later credit Roy's influence for their success. Again, while Jacques Plante was one of the first goalies to roam from his net to handle pucks and aid his defensemen, Roy took the role of the puck-handling goalie to a new level.

Today's NHL goalie often acts as a third defenseman, using league rules which prohibit players from checking goaltenders when they stray from their crease, to go out and handle the puck at will. Goalies have also become excellent shooters, capable of sending the puck 200 feet down the ice into the opposition net when the goalie has been pulled for an extra attacker late in a game.

With today's NHL game faster than ever, techniques are always being improved. Where once goaltenders used to put their foot up when making a glove or pad save, today's goaltenders are taught to keep their foot down, which allows the pad to stay on the ground, thus preventing shots from sliding underneath them.

"I'd say that is the biggest single change in the last 10 years," says Mitch Korn, goaltending coach of the Nashville Predators. "That and going down. Now, it's not a question of whether a goalie should go down. It's when and how."

The butterfly technique now includes the half-butterfly—a move where the goaltender goes down and only moves one pad out to his right or left. As Korn explains, the half-butterfly has all but eliminated stacked-pad saves. "It's all about getting to the puck quicker," he says. "And a half-butterfly gets you there quicker than sliding across and having to stack your pads. I teach eight different half-butterfly techniques."

Korn is just one of many goaltending coaches employed by NHL teams today. Besides offering invaluable "psychological" assistance to a team's goalie, the goaltending coach also keeps an eye on technique. Is the goalie going down too quickly? Is he reading the plays properly? Is his catching glove positioned properly? His blocker? Is he giving the shooter too much five-hole? Are his angles solid?

A goaltending coach is constantly reinforcing the fundamentals of the position. And with video analysis, deficiencies can be spotted and corrected in practice. This is just another reason why goaltending today is stronger than it has been in any other era of the NHL.

And with today's NHL goaltenders grabbing more and more of the spotlight—Dominik Hasek, with his headline-making back-to-back league MVP awards and five Vezina trophies, for instance—the position has also never been more attractive to kids playing the game. No wonder today's best young athletes are turning to one of the most pressure-packed positions in pro sports. No doubt these future goaltenders will take the position to new heights, just as Hasek, Eddie Belfour, Curtis Joseph and others played the game better than the goalies of the 1980s.

New York Islanders prospect Roberto Luongo, the highest-drafted goalie—fourth overall in 1997—in NHL history, represents the next wave of goaltenders entering the league.

At six-foot-three Luongo not only has the big frame that NHL teams appear to like today, but he has all the mental and physical tools as well. Like so many developing young goaltenders, Luongo had many influences and coaches that have helped him fashion a technique that incorporates the styles of many of the game's top backstoppers.

In the NHL's most recent draft, another goalie—Brian Finley of the Ontario Hockey League's Barrie Colts—was taken fifth overall by the Nashville Predators. The big, six-foot-two, 180-pounder from Sault Ste. Marie, Ontario, is another of the new breed that will dominate the position over the next 10 to 15 years.

"What we're about to see is a huge turnover among the league's goaltenders," says Korn. "There is a new generation of goalies who will be entering the league, taking over from the older goalies in the league right now."

A new generation of trendsetters, who, in their own way, will change the position in ways we can't even imagine.

Martin Brodeur

30 NEW JERSEY DEVILS

Martin Brodeur knows what they say about his kind. About people who don 40 pounds of equipment every night to get pelted by rock-hard pieces of rubber.

He's heard, often enough, that his brain must be as hard as the pucks players shoot at him; what else could explain a desire to skate out on an ice surface with the job of defending the net? How else could you explain someone who routinely stares down someone 15 feet away, their hockey stick pulled back like a slingshot, waiting to launch a tiny black missile at 100 mph?

Right at your head.

Yep, Martin Brodeur has heard it all. Not surprisingly, the affable New Jersey netminder's take on goaltending is a little bit different. His perspective, shall we say, is at odds with just about everyone else's.

"I know some people think we're stupid," Brodeur says. "But I don't know. What about the guy who has to go get the puck when Eric Lindros is coming in at him 100 mph. Who's crazier, me or him?

"Look, I've got a mask. I don't have any stitches. I've got my teeth. So if one of my kids wants to be a goalie, great. I think it's a little bit safer than forward or defense." And then Martin Brodeur begins to laugh.

If you're looking for someone who breaks the goalie stereotype, looking

for someone who doesn't need to draw a cone of silence around him before a game, do his skate laces up a certain way before heading out on the ice, tap his pads an exact number of times before the referee drops the puck, Martin Brodeur is your man. He's as normal as they come.

"I'm just having fun," Brodeur says, when asked to explain his ever easy-going disposition, regardless of the pressure.

And it shows on the ice. Take a look behind Brodeur's mask, and you'll more often find one of the NHL's top goaltender's smiling, then grimacing in concentration. Looking for someone to attach a microphone to during an NHL all-star game? Brodeur will be the first to stick up his hand. And he'll make the television producers even happier by singing during the game.

Don't get the wrong idea. There's nothing lightweight about Brodeur's abilities. At the young age of 27, the kid from Montreal has already won a Vezina Trophy, the CalderTrophy as the league's top rookie, and, most importantly,

a Stanley Cup. After only six seasons, Brodeur already has 201 victories. Amazing.

Brodeur, of course, had goaltending in his genes. He just didn't realize it right away.

His father, Denis, played goal for the Canadian national team and represented his country at the 1956 Olympics where Canada finished with a bronze medal. But young Martin wouldn't discover his father's link to the position until after he had chosen it for himself.

Which is a story in itself.

As a youngster, Martin Brodeur played for two hockey teams. On one, he was a forward, on the other, a goalie.

He liked both positions. His mother preferred him to play out. She enjoyed watching her son score goals. But then one day Brodeur's coach issued an ultimatum.

"Martin, what are you going to play? Goalie or forward?"

Young Martin wasn't expecting the question. Today, Brodeur remembers the moment

like it was yesterday. "I freaked out and said: 'Okay, goalie.'"

And that was it.

"It was kind of weird," Brodeur says. "Destiny is in your hands and you don't even know it."

Brodeur demonstrated an affinity for the position from the beginning. But he wasn't always the best in the area where he grew up. In fact, Brodeur would be cut from the Bantam all-star team, a sign to many that their NHL dreams are over.

Which is what Martin Brodeur figured. But destiny had other plans.

Discouraged and disillusioned, Brodeur had a conversation with his older brother, who convinced his young sibling not to give up. To use the experience as motivation.

He did.

Brodeur would go on to have a solid amateur career with St. Hyacinthe of the Quebec Major Junior League. Fate would be on his side again when Brodeur was drafted by the defense-minded New Jersey Devils. The Devils, under the then-guidance of coach Jacques Lemaire, played a defense-first, tight-checking, low-mistake style of hockey. If their goalie faced more than 20 shots a night, then the team wasn't doing its job. It was the perfect system for a young goalie to break into.

"Well, it gave me a lot of confidence, that's for sure," says Brodeur. "It makes a big difference for a goalie to go out and play for a good team.

"You play under pressure all the time. People want you to win, win, win and do well all the

time. And with this team you knew you weren't going to face 50 shots and get hung out to dry all the time."

Nevertheless, Brodeur did play in many games with scores of 1-0 or 2-1, when one bad goal could cost his team a victory. And yet, Brodeur has been able to maintain a cool and calm demeanor no matter how high the intensity gauge is set.

"I tend to look at the big picture rather than one game," says Brodeur. "I tend not to get overwhelmed by one performance either way. It helps me get through stretches that are better and stretches that are harder."

Still, you have to wonder: if baseball's Larry Walker can confess that he's scared of Houston pitcher Randy Johnson's fastball, won't Brodeur concede that he isn't as cool and calm when St. Louis' Al MacInnis is winding up for a slapshot?

Isn't fear a legitimate fact of a goaltender's life?

Well, first Brodeur will tell you that when it comes to the hardest shots in the NHL, Al MacInnis is in a "league of his own." But don't expect Brodeur to admit that he's shaking in his goalie skates when Big Al's shot is heading towards him.

"You can't be scared," says Brodeur. "Maybe there are some goalies who are, but the better the guy, the better the challenge is for me.

"If you start fearing them you'll be out of the league for sure."

Now, while Brodeur may not be as quirky as some goalies past and present, he does have this thing about soap operas. Particularly "Days of Our Lives."

It's part of his secret life.

You see, it's extremely important for Brodeur

to watch the popular soap opera every day. On game days, he'll watch the show and then have a nap. But not for more than two hours. If Brodeur dozes for any longer than that, he's too tired for the game. After waking up, he'll chow down a small snack, like a banana or chocolate bar and he's ready to go.

Now, you're probably asking, what happens on weekends when "Days of Our Lives" isn't on? Brodeur says: "What I try to do is find something else on the tube that catches my attention, but nothing can match my soap. What it comes down to is being in the best frame of mind for the game."

While 1998–99 wasn't Brodeur's best year statis-

tically, he still boasted a goals against average of 2.29 a stat most goalies would kill for. Brodeur's Devils finished first overall in the eastern conference, but they were upset in the first round of the playoffs by Pittsburgh.

Brodeur, of course, has had several statistically satisfying years. In 1996-97, Brodeur's GAA of 1.88 was the lowest in the NHL since 1971-72. Young Brodeur got a good look at life in the NHL thanks to his father, Denis, who was and remains the official photographer of the Montreal Canadiens. Denis would pay his young son $5 to help carry his camera equipment to the arena for photo shoots and team practices.

"My dad would talk to players like Claude Lemieux and Stephane Richer and tell them one day his son was going to play in the NHL," Brodeur said of two players who would later become teammates in New Jersey.

"How many dads say the same thing? But, gee, he was right."

Young Martin also got a chance to study his goalie hero, Patrick Roy, upclose. "Everyone always looked up to him," Brodeur said. "I said I wanted a picture of my favorite goalies and my dad made kind of a frame of all these guys. Now I'm playing against them."

Yes, Martin Brodeur has come a long way. He and wife, Melanie, have a three-year-old, Anthony, and two-year-old twins, William and Jeremy. Goaltending, it seems, is already in the blood of at least one of the Brodeur children.

"We have a big rec room with two nets in it and Anthony is always wanting me to take shots on him," Brodeur says, his eyes brightening when he talks about his children.

"When I come home from practice he wants me to take shots. When he gets up from his nap, he wants shots."

And how would he like it if his boy decided he wanted to be an NHL goalie one day, just like his dad?

"I would love it, for sure."

Martin Brodeur is the kind of guy who'd like everyone to have a chance to chase a dream. It's precisely for that reason that Brodeur shelled out $104,000 to have an ice rink built in St. Leboire, Quebec, the small town where he played junior hockey. "I lived in Montreal all my life, and everything was accessible to me," he says, explaining why he built the Martin Brodeur Center. " But if you live in a town where there are 3,500 people and everything is 15 to 20 minutes away to drive, there's not much you can do in that town. A center like this keeps the young kids out of trouble."

			REGULAR SEASON								PLAYOFFS						
Year	Team	Lea	GP	W	L	T	Mins	GA	SO	Avg	GP	W	L	Mins	GA	SO	Avg
1989-90	St.-Hyacinthe	QMJHL	42	23	13	2	2333	156	0	4.01	12	5	7	678	46	0	4.07
1990-91	St.-Hyacinthe	QMJHL	52	22	24	4	2946	162	2	3.30	4	0	4	232	16	0	4.14
1991-92	New Jersey	NHL	4	2	1	0	179	10	0	3.35	1	0	1	32	3	0	5.63
	St.-Hyacinthe	QMJHL	48	27	16	4	2846	161	2	3.39	5	2	3	317	14	0	2.65
1992-93	Utica	AHL	32	14	13	5	1952	131	0	4.03	4	1	3	258	18	0	4.19
1993-94	New Jersey	NHL	47	27	11	8	2625	105	3	2.40	17	8	9	1171	38	1	1.95
1994-95	New Jersey	NHL	40	19	11	6	2184	89	3	2.45	20	16	4	1222	34	3	1.67
1995-96	New Jersey	NHL	77	34	30	12	4433	173	6	2.34	....	....	....	....	....	....	....
1996-97	New Jersey	NHL	67	37	14	13	3838	120	10	1.88	10	5	5	659	19	2	1.73
	Canada	W Cup	2	0	1	0	60	4	0	4.00	....	....	....	....	....	....	....
1997-98	New Jersey	NHL	70	43	17	8	4128	130	10	1.89	6	2	4	366	12	0	1.97
	Canada	Olympics					DID NOT PLAY - SPARE GOALTENDER										
1998-99	New Jersey	NHL	70	39	21	10	4239	162	4	2.29	7	3	4	425	20	0	2.82

Byron Dafoe

34 BOSTON BRUINS

It was the spring of 1971. The baby, the son of a British mother and a Canadian father, was just three months old.

The infant's mother, Jane Dafoe, wanted to bring her child to Canada, but the immigration officer wasn't making it easy.

"I don't know what it was," recalls the boy, who's now a 195-pound, 28-year-old adult. "But some of the paperwork wasn't right. There was some delay or something.

"Finally, the guy just let her through—and no lie, this is what he said: 'Aw, go ahead. We'll let him in. He looks like a hockey player.' "

It's a story Byron Dafoe is fond of telling. For not only did he end up playing hockey, he also made it to the National Hockey League, where he proved to be a formidable goaltender.

Dafoe—his mom named him after Lord Byron, the English romantic poet—was born in Sussex, England, but grew up in British Columbia. He played junior hock-

ey with the WHL, then joined the ECHL and finally the AHL, where he tended net for New Haven and Baltimore. In other words, by the time Dafoe made it to the big leagues—he was drafted by Washington in 1989, right behind his good friend, Olaf Kolzig—he had truly paid his dues.

Looking back, Dafoe says he never lost sight of the ultimate goal. "I wouldn't say there was one particular moment when I didn't aspire to be here, or that I lost my drive to be in the NHL."

Dafoe's involvement with the Capitals was thin, at best. He played just 10 games for the Caps before being traded to Los Angeles in 1995, where for two seasons he proved himself to be a strong, acrobatic goaltender who happened to be hugely popular with the fans. But on August 29, 1997, the love-in ended: that was the day Dafoe received a call telling him that he and Dmitri Khristich had been dealt to the Boston Bruins in a deal that sent Jozef Stumpel and Sandy Moger the other way.

At first, Dafoe was disappointed with the news. He adored California, and he'd just bought himself a house on the beach. But it didn't take long for him to change his point of view and warm up to Boston.

> It is the mental aspect of hockey, argues Dafoe, that ultimately distinguishes the good goaltender from the great.

"It's such a great hockey city," he says. "In L.A., there's so much going on you kind of get lost in the crowd. But here it's all hockey. If you do well, it's a great place to play."

Dafoe has done well, indeed. In his first season he worked his way into the No. 1 slot, and ended up with a 30-25-9 record and a goals-against average of 2.24. Last year, the stats were just as impressive. Dafoe won 32 games and posted a GAA of 1.99.

Dafoe, as hockey-watchers well know, is not a goalie whose style can be easily categorized. Most, however, describe him as a stand-up goalie who favors the butterfly, an unconventional, cerebral sort who uses his head as much as his reflexes.

"I have to challenge and be aggressive," says Dafoe. "I try not to get too floppy."

But according to Dafoe, the physical game is just half the battle. Since the age of 17, he's also done considerable mental training: before every game, and even between periods of games, he visualizes what might happen.

"In the afternoons, I just mentally run through the game, visualize myself making the saves, patting the guys on the head after a victory. . . . Hey, the mind is a powerful thing. And we don't tap into it enough."

It is the mental aspect of hockey, argues Dafoe, that ultimately distin-guishes the good goaltender from the great.

"I think at this level, everyone can play, but the guys who become great are the ones who are very strong-minded and mentally prepared for games. The Patrick Roys and Andy Moogs, who've survived all these years and been so successful."

Dafoe, who tossed off all his superstitions four years ago, is no more stereotypical off the ice than he is on it. Here is a guy who not only likes to play golf and tennis, but also enjoys training German police dogs. (Dafoe has even been known to dress up in protective gear at dog shows and let himself be attacked by other people's police dogs. "To have a 120-pound Schutzund German shepherd come at you is unbelievable," he says.)

No, in no way is Byron Dafoe your average sort of guy. And that, it is clear, suits the Boston Bruins just fine.

> "In the afternoons, I just mentally run through the game, visualize myself making the saves, patting the guys on the head after a victory . . . . Hey, the mind is a pow-erful thing. And we don't tap into it enough."

"He's the ultimate competitor," says former Bruins goalie Gerry Cheevers. "I think he's there. I think he's with the big boys now. He's the type of guy that players can look at and say 'OK, we've got a pretty good guy going for us.' I think that's important."

At first glance, Byron Dafoe appears to have little in common with an 18th-century Romantic poet. Take another look, though, and you'll notice the words "Lord Byron" on the bottom of his mask—a reference to the celebrated and colorful English poet after whom Dafoe is named. "It was my mom," explains Dafoe. "She named me after him because she read a lot of his poetry. His work is very popular in Britain." What, then, of the names on the back of his mask? Are Vamp and Zona also poets?

Not a chance: those are Dafoe's beloved German shepherds.

Year	Team	Lea	REGULAR SEASON								PLAYOFFS						
			GP	W	L	T	Mins	GA	SO	Avg	GP	W	L	Mins	GA	SO	Avg
1988-89	Portland	WHL	59	29	24	3	3279	291	1	5.32	18	10	8	1091	81	1	4.45
1989-90	Washington	Fr Tour	2	....	....	....	60	3	0	3.00							
	Portland	WHL	40	14	21	3	2265	193	0	5.11	....	....	....	....	....	....	....
1990-91	Portland	WHL	8	1	5	1	414	41	0	5.94	....	....	....	....	....	....	....
	Prince Albert	WHL	32	13	12	4	1839	124	0	4.05	....	....	....	....	....	....	....
1991-92	Baltimore	AHL	33	12	16	4	1847	119	0	3.87							
	New Haven	AHL	7	3	2	1	364	22	0	3.63	....	....	....	....	....	....	....
	Hampton	ECHL	10	6	4	0	562	26	0	2.78	....	....	....	....	....	....	....
1992-93	Washington	NHL	1	0	0	0	1	0	0	0.00	....	....	....	....	....	....	....
	Baltimore	AHL	48	16	20	7	2617	191	1	4.38	5	2	3	241	22	0	5.48
1993-94	Washington	NHL	5	2	2	0	230	13	0	3.39	2	0	2	118	5	0	2.54
	Portland	AHL	47	24	16	4	2661	148	1	3.34	1	0	0	9	1	0	6.79
1994-95	Phoenix	IHL	49	25	16	6	2743	169	2	3.70	....	....	....	....	....	....	....
	Washington	NHL	4	1	1	1	187	11	0	3.53	1	0	0	20	1	0	3.00
	Portland	AHL	6	5	0	0	330	16	0	2.91	7	3	4	416	29	0	4.18
1995-96	Los Angeles	NHL	47	14	24	8	2666	172	1	3.87	....	....	....	....	....	....	....
1996-97	Los Angeles	NHL	40	13	17	5	2162	112	0	3.11	....	....	....	....	....	....	....
1997-98	Boston	NHL	65	30	25	9	3693	138	6	2.24	6	2	4	422	14	1	1.99
1998-99	Boston	NHL	68	32	23	11	4001	133	10	1.99	12	6	6	768	26	2	2.03

John Vanbiesbrouck

34 PHILADELPHIA FLYERS

When it comes to tending a hockey net, it's the little things that make a difference. And in the case of John Vanbiesbrouck, the little things are everything.

You won't be treated to breathtaking acrobatics when The Beezer's between the pipes. You won't be watching high-jumps or belly flops or superhuman displays of agility.

John Vanbiesbrouck is not as interested in putting on a show as he is in writing the script. And most nights, he ensures it has a happy ending.

Last season, he guarded the posts in 62 games for the Philadelphia Flyers, finishing with 27 wins, 18 losses and 15 ties. He recorded 6 shutouts and posted a goals-against average of 2.18.

And true to his style, he scarcely flapped his wings. "He made a lot of big saves," says Flyers' coach Roger Neilson. "Often, they don't look like big saves. He's in the right position all the time."

Vanbiesbrouck is what's known as a goaltending minimalist. He moves when necessary, but only then. He's Mr. Anti-Flash, a netminder who's out to stop the puck, and not necessarily to make a pretty save.

"I try not to overreact to the puck," he says. "You are going to make mistakes, but you try to limit them.

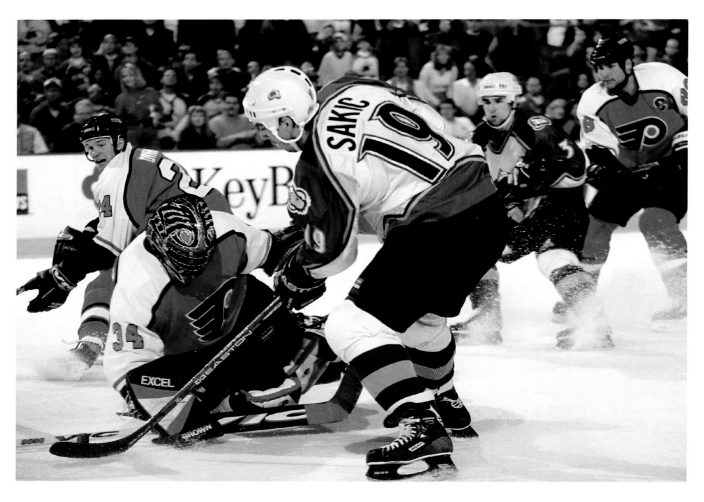

"In this game, half the battle is making the puck hit you. Actually, it could be the whole battle."

The effect, of course, is one of calmness and control. And when it comes to the Flyers, it's a feeling that's infectious.

Defenseman Eric Desjardins says the netminder simply refuses to get rattled. "It can be very frustrating to play against him and see he's always calm and making it look easy.

"It makes everyone else play a little bit more relaxed, with more confidence, because you know he's back there to cover for you. It's great to have him on our side."

Eric Lindros, who captains the Philadelphia team, says The Beezer has had a positive influence on the entire club ever since he was picked up from the Florida Panthers in 1998.

"What he provides is a calming effect," says Lindros. "He's allowed our defense to play with more confidence. And I think that is flowing out to the forwards, too."

Vanbiesbrouck, who's 36, has been guarding the nets—and calming his teams—for an awfully long time. The Detroit native had to beg his parents to let him play goal when he was just seven years old, and learned by watching his older brother Frank, who had also gravitated toward the goalie net.

"I basically learned by watching him and other guys," recalls Vanbiesbrouck, who never attended a goalie school or camp.

Vanbiesbrouck spent his junior years with

> "In this game, half the battle is making the puck hit you. Actually, it could be the whole battle.

the Sault Ste. Marie Greyhounds of the Ontario Hockey League, and in 1980–81 was awarded the Dinty Moore Trophy for being the rookie with the lowest GAA.

It was also in 1981 that Vanbiesbrouck advanced to the world of professional hockey. He was drafted by the New York Rangers, and on December 5, 1981, at the age of 18, played his first National Hockey League game, turning aside 30 shots to lift the Rangers to a 2-1 victory over the Colorado Rockies.

In the 11 seasons Vanbiesbrouck played with the Rangers, his best season was in 1985–86 when he recorded 31 regular-season wins and led the Rangers to the Stanley Cup semifinals. That year he also won the Vezina Trophy for outstanding netminding.

In 1993–94, No. 34 moved to the Florida Panthers, then newcomers to the NHL. Craig Ramsay, who was an assistant coach with the Panthers that year, remembers how impressed he was with Vanbiesbrouck, who was the only recognizable name on the team.

"He was thrown behind a whole group of players who were trying to find out who they were. Now that's pressure. He stepped up and said, 'I'm the guy.' "

Among goalies, The Guy is a definite standout. He has no superstitions—unlike many of his counterparts—and is the complete opposite of the stereotypical wacky goaltender. He is, however, a balanced kind of guy, an articulate, grounded family man who says the highlight of his day comes when he picks up his three sons at school.

Clearly, there's a sense of balance in Vanbiesbrouck's life, and he knows exactly when it was planted: in 1993, when his brother Frank died. The experience, as devastating as it was, pulled Vanbiesbrouck closer to his family and helped him to mature and develop a better sense of purpose.

These days, those who know John Vanbiesbrouck will tell you that he's a pretty normal guy, a relaxed, poised athlete whose brainpower is his biggest strength.

"There's a different kind of mental toughness required of a goalie," says sports psychologist Joel H. Fish, who works with the Flyers. "And John Vanbiesbrouck is at the highest level of mental toughness of any athlete I've been around."

To say John Vanbiesbrouck is unusually cool for a goalie is a major understatement. Not only does The Beezer fail to get rattled before a game—he sometimes forgets to even think about it. Last season, for instance, he was driving to the rink one night when he began to focus on his son's upcoming science project. "I thought of all the things he needed to do in order to prepare for it," says Vanbiesbrouck. "I found myself worrying more about his stuff, while he's probably more worried about how I'm going to play. Things like that help me keep the job in perspective."

			REGULAR SEASON								PLAYOFFS						
Year	Team	Lea	GP	W	L	T	Mins	GA	SO	Avg	GP	W	L	Mins	GA	SO	Avg
1980-81	Sault Ste. Marie	OHA	56	31	16	1	2941	203	0	4.14	11	3	3	457	24	1	3.15
1981-82	N.Y. Rangers	NHL	1	1	0	0	60	1	0	1.00	....	....	....	....	....	....	....
	Sault Ste. Marie	OHL	31	12	12	2	1686	102	0	3.62	7	1	4	276	20	0	4.35
	United States	WJC-A	5	1	3	0	200	19	0	5.70	....	....	....	....	....	....	....
1982-83	Sault Ste. Marie	OHL	62	39	21	1	3471	209	0	3.61	16	7	6	944	56	1	3.56
	United States	WJC-A	5	....	....	....	280	17	....	3.64	....	....	....	....	....	....	....
1983-84	N.Y. Rangers	NHL	3	2	1	0	180	10	0	3.33	1	0	0	1	0	0	0.00
	Tulsa Oilers	CHL	37	20	13	2	2153	124	3	3.46	4	4	0	240	10	0	2.50
1984-85	N.Y. Rangers	NHL	42	12	24	3	2358	166	1	4.22	1	0	0	20	0	0	0.00
	United States	WEC-A	9	6	3	0	492	46	....	5.64	....	....	....	....	....	....	....
1985-86	N.Y. Rangers	NHL	61	31	21	5	3326	184	3	3.32	16	8	8	899	49	1	3.27
1986-87	N.Y. Rangers	NHL	50	18	20	5	2656	161	0	3.64	4	1	3	195	11	1	3.38
	United States	WEC-A	7	2	5	0	419	28	....	4.01	....	....	....	....	....	....	....
1987-88	United States	C Cup	4	2	2	0	240	9	....	2.00	....	....	....	....	....	....	....
	N.Y. Rangers	NHL	56	27	22	7	3319	187	2	3.38	....	....	....	....	....	....	....
1988-89	N.Y. Rangers	NHL	56	28	21	4	3207	197	0	3.69	2	0	1	107	6	0	3.36
	United States	WEC-A	5	....	....	....	....	20	....	4.53	....	....	....	....	....	....	....
1989-90	N.Y. Rangers	NHL	47	19	19	7	2734	154	1	3.38	6	2	3	298	15	0	3.02
1990-91	N.Y. Rangers	NHL	40	15	18	6	2257	126	3	3.35	1	0	0	52	1	0	1.15
	United States	WEC-A	10	....	....	....	....	41	....	4.67	....	....	....	....	....	....	....
1991-92	United States	C Cup	1	1	0	0	60	3	0	3.00	....	....	....	....	....	....	....
	N.Y. Rangers	NHL	45	27	13	3	2526	120	2	2.85	7	2	5	368	23	0	3.75
1992-93	N.Y. Rangers	NHL	48	20	18	7	2757	152	4	3.31	....	....	....	....	....	....	....
1993-94	Florida	NHL	57	21	25	11	3440	145	1	2.53	....	....	....	....	....	....	....
1994-95	Florida	NHL	37	14	15	4	2087	86	4	2.47	....	....	....	....	....	....	....
1995-96	Florida	NHL	57	26	20	7	3178	142	2	2.68	22	12	10	1332	50	1	2.25
1996-97	Florida	NHL	57	27	19	10	3347	128	2	2.29	5	1	4	328	13	1	2.38
1997-98	Florida	NHL	60	18	29	11	3451	165	4	2.87	....	....	....	....	....	....	....
	United States	Olympics	1	0	0	0	1	0	0	0.00	....	....	....	....	....	....	....
1998-99	Philadelphia	NHL	62	27	18	15	3712	135	6	2.18	6	2	4	369	9	1	1.46

Psyche

Sometimes it would strike in the middle of a game. An opposing player would be flying down the wing towards him, and Glen Hanlon would be overcome with panic.

"I would just get hit with this feeling that I couldn't stop the puck," remembers Hanlon, describing moments he had as a goalie in a successful 14-year NHL career.

"I could be in the middle of a great game, and I'd have really good thoughts, and all of a sudden another thought process would take over and then someone would shoot a puck from the blue line and I wouldn't be sure that I could stop it."

Welcome inside the mind of an NHL goalie.

Few positions in all of sport are as mentally taxing as that of a goaltender. One minute you're brimming with confidence, the next you're imagining every shot going between your legs. One game you're the first star, the next you're being fingered for the loss.

There are enormous burdens that come with being your team's last line of defense. Weighty psychological baggage too. Put yourself in a goalie's position. Your team is ahead by one goal. There is one minute left in the game when an opposing forward gets a breakaway. And all of a sudden 19,000 hometown fans are on their feet.

Stop the puck and you're a hero. Let it in, and the groans are deafening.

It takes a rare bird to play a position that comes with that kind of responsibility. A place on the ice that often comes with as much heartbreak and sorrow as joy and happiness.

"Playing goal is not fun," Hall of Fame goaltender Ken Dryden once said. "Behind a mask, there are no smiling faces, nor timely, sweaty grins of satisfaction. It is a grim, humorless position . . . it is only when a game [ends] and the mask comes off, when the immense challenge of the job turns abruptly to immense satisfaction or despair, that the unsmiling grimness lifts and goes away."

Not surprisingly, the psychological makeup of a goaltender has generally been regarded as being different than that of forwards and defensemen. While all prepare for games in their own individual way, goalies have often been found to be more aloof, a little quieter than the rest of their teammates, in the hours leading up to a game.

"When I prepared for a game, I didn't allow my mind to rest," the great Russian goaltender Vladislav Tretiak said. "I thought about ways to play better, analyzed the strong and weak points of the opposing team and drew up plans of action."

Tretiak would become unusually pensive on game days, often finding peace and solace by repeating the mantra: "I am a goalie. I have a special responsibility. I am not allowed to make mistakes." On the way from the dressing room to the ice, he would not hear anyone speaking to him, so intense was his concentration.

Not everyone, of course, prepares for games quite like this. New Jersey Devils goalie Martin Brodeur can be downright chatty in the hours leading up to a game. For Brodeur, the less he thinks about the game and all the pressure that

comes with it, the more relaxed he is when he skates out on the ice.

Patrick Roy of the Colorado Avalanche, like many goaltenders past and present, finds internal peace through routine and ritual, including putting on his equipment in precisely the same order before each game, bouncing a puck on the floor in front of him, and then always laying it on the ground to his right side.

"The rituals just help me," said Roy. "I don't know why or how they all got started, but they just help put me at ease and give me some comfort before the game."

Former NHL goalie Kelly Hrudey, now a hockey commentator, didn't even mind doing interviews on game days. But he would grow quieter in the hours before the game, as he went through a mental checklist of the things he needed to do on the ice.

Hanlon, whose NHL career included stops in Vancouver, St. Louis, New York with the Rangers and Detroit, tried both ways of preparing for games.

"When I first started my career, I removed myself from everything," Hanlon remembers. "I had everything regimented from the second I woke up. I wouldn't talk to anybody. I wouldn't listen to anything. I knew what time I'd have to be home to nap. What I was going to eat."

But eventually, Hanlon found his routine too exacting. He thought so much about the game, he sometimes "psyched himself out" thinking about everything he had to do,

> "The rituals just help me," said Roy. "I don't know why or how they all got started, but they just help put me at ease and give me some comfort before the game."

the shooters he had to face. So he decided to change.

"I tried to make the day as normal as possible," said Hanlon, now the head coach of the Portland Pirates of the American Hockey League. "I tried thinking less about the game, not more." Still, it would be impossible not to have a range of emotions throughout the day. At nine a.m. he was going to get a shutout. An hour later, he was going to let everything in.

"So from the time you woke up to the time you actually played the game, you've had 100 great games and 100 bad ones. You were just hoping that by game time, when the dice finally stopped rolling, you were having a great game, not a bad one."

To be sure, the mental gymnastics don't stop for a goalie once he skates out on to the ice. In some cases, it's only the beginning. Any pre-game doubts a goalie may have can sometimes be exacerbated by an early goal by the other team. Conversely, a big save can often fuel him with enough confidence to last throughout the game.

While many netminders allow goals—especially those considered stoppable, known in the hockey vernacular as "soft"—to eat away at their psyche, great ones like Tretiak found ways to erase the memory of the puck behind him as quickly as it happened.

"I never tried to understand why it happened," said Tretiak. "The analysis came after the game. I tried to regain my composure as quickly as possible and told myself, 'It's nothing. I'm playing well.' "

Still, no matter how well prepared a goaltender is, no matter how great the career is that he's enjoying, there are moments in every netminder's life that are, well, inexplicable. When his mind is simply overwhelmed by the unique forces that exert themselves on this position.

"I had one instance in my career where I was really baffled," longtime NHL goalie Andy Moog remembers. "John Ogrodnick was driving down the wing and he took a shot. The puck literally vanished on me. I had no idea where it was.

"There was no screen, no deflection. There was nothing between him and me—but after he took the shot, the next time I saw that puck it was behind me in the net. It was the first time in my career that I was totally baffled."

It is after moments like these, after bad goals that have cost your team the game, that it is nice for a goaltender to have someone to talk to. Someone to help ease the frustration and despair, the mental anguish that a goaltender feels more strongly than his teammates.

Until the late 1980s, goaltenders only had friends and family to turn to for comfort and understanding. And while they could offer soothing words, it was often cold comfort to the goalie whose picture was in the paper under some headline that included the word "goat."

Enter the goalie coach.

As much as he's been brought into the NHL picture to help refine a goaltender's technique, the goalie coach is also part psychologist. Possessing a unique knowledge and understanding of the position and all the demons that can erode a netminder's confidence, the goalie coach can offer more than just kind words to help give his player a psychological boost. He

Almost as certain as the relief an NHL goalie feels when he finally hangs up his skates, is the likelihood that his retirement from professional hockey will include a career as a hockey commentator.

More and more, television networks have sought out former NHL goaltenders to be part of their broadcast teams covering hockey.

Former Ranger standout John Davidson is perhaps the most high-profile ex-goalie who has moved into the broadcast booth. But by no means is he alone. Former Blackhawk goalie Darren Pang does commentary for ESPN, while Kelly Hrudey, who played for the Los Angeles Kings, New York Islanders and San Jose Sharks, provides color analysis for the CBC in Canada.

Toronto Maple Leaf backup Glenn Healy has also done some television work, as has former Vancouver Canucks goalie John Garrett. Greg Millen, who played for six NHL teams in a 14-year career, provides analysis for CTV's SportsNet in Canada.

"Being a goalie, you spend a lot of time with the media during your career, for starters," says Millen, explaining why so many of his netminding colleagues later find themselves in broadcasting.

"When no one's around, the media always head for the goalie. So, you're comfortable with the media to begin with."

Millen says a goaltender also has a rare vantage point not afforded to other players on the team. Throughout his career, he sees the game unfold in front of him. As his team skates down the ice, the goalie not only sees what his teammates are doing, but what the opponents are doing to combat any attack.

"Therefore, you tend to analyze things," says Millen. "It's part of your nature. Part of your personality."

And, most goalies will be quick to tell you, they're generally smarter and more articulate than their colleagues playing defense and forward. Then again, they might be a little biased.

can offer intelligent analysis of the goalie's game and give constructive advice. Something a goalie can understand. Something that is tangible. And, most importantly, something that helps the goalie turn his attention almost immediately to improving his performance rather than dwelling on his mistakes.

Goaltending coaches such as Nashville's Mitch Korn, New Jersey's Jacques Caron and Anaheim's Francois Allaire, have also come to provide an important link between the goaltender and the head coach, who often

> **Possessing a unique knowledge and understanding of the position and all the demons that can erode a netminder's confidence, the goalie coach can offer more than just kind words to help give his player a psychological boost.**

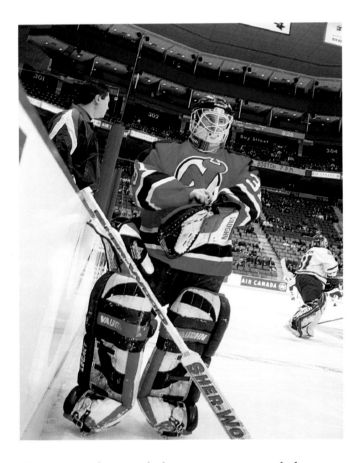

armpits, so I couldn't go down," remembers longtime NHL goalie Gary "Suitcase" Smith. "Then he'd let players come in and shoot on me. The idea was to get me to stand up more on shots instead of going down. That's how they worked on technique back then [in the early 1960s]."

You can imagine all the good that drill did. Smith, who at the time was not yet wearing a mask, was often terrified when the ropes came out and the pucks started flying. And he'd end up an emotional basketcase afterwards.

Coaches today would no more think of tying their goalies to the net than they would consider firing pistols at their forwards to get them to skate faster. If anything, NHL coaches now go out of their way to ensure that their goalies are happy. Anything they can do to put their backstopper's mind at ease, they'll do, it would seem.

"All I know is, I wish I was pampered as much as Eddie [Belfour] is pampered," said Dallas Stars forward Brett Hull. "Boy, what Eddie wants, Eddie gets. It must be nice, I'll tell you."

As much as changes in equipment over the years have allowed goaltenders to become more mobile and have enhanced performance, they have also had a profound impact on the psychological makeup of the person playing the position.

Once upon a time, along with dealing with the usual emotional highs and lows that come with the position, goaltenders had to deal with the "terror" of 90-mph slapshots with little protection, especially for their face. However, the advances in equipment that have now made goaltending possibly the safest position in hockey, have also been a psychological boon to the person playing the position.

doesn't understand the unique mental dynamics involved in playing the position.

"I talk to my goal coach more than I talk to my head coach," says New Jersey backstopper Martin Brodeur. "It's kind of like a pipeline between the coaches and myself. The goalie gets to know what's going on and how the coaches feel about you." Which is important.

There was a time, not that long ago, that a coach had little time or regard for the psychological care or condition of his goaltender. In fact, coaches quite often did more harm than good.

"I remember in Rochester [of the American Hockey League], the coach used to strap me to the net with ropes, just under the

> **Coaches today would no more think of tying their goalies to the net than they would consider firing pistols at their forwards to get them to skate faster.**

But even with the advances in equipment, even with their own personal psychologists disguised as goalie coaches, there will always be a loneliness, a nakedness, that is associated with the goalie position.

"I became a lot braver," said Andy Moog. "The puck didn't hurt anymore. I wasn't frightened. I was frightened the first half of my career. But I wasn't in my second half. So it really changed my [mental] outlook."

But even with the advances in equipment, even with their own personal psychologists disguised as goalie coaches, there will always be a loneliness, a nakedness, that is associated with the goaltending position.

While he may practice hard on his technique, nothing can really prepare a goaltender for the jolt to his psyche every time the red light goes off behind him. A goaltender is often the object of the fans' wrath more than any other player on a hockey team. Ten great games can be wiped out by one bad one. Forty great saves forgotten after one soft goal.

He skates out on the ice for every game, carrying the weight of his team's fortunes on his shoulders. The tiniest slipup becomes obvious to all—because usually it means the puck is in the net behind him.

It's a celebrated position to be sure. There can be glorious wins that you are responsible for. But there can also be miserable losses that can drive a stake through your heart. It takes a special person to find comfort between the pipes. A special mind too.

"Every goalie will have some sort of mental meltdown at some point," says Hanlon. "It's going to hit you. It's just a matter of when. The key is learning how to handle it. That often differentiates the great goalies from the ones who have less success.

"Goaltending," Hanlon says, "is all mental."

Curtis Joseph

31 TORONTO MAPLE LEAFS

Meet Curtis Joseph, and you start to believe in fate.

Listen to his story and hear about the obstacles that once stood between a kid and a career in the National Hockey League, and you start to think that, yes, some things really are meant to be.

After all, Curtis Joseph did not simply have to jump a few hurdles to get where he is: inside the crease for the Toronto Maple Leafs. He had to soar high above them, again and again and again.

On more than one occasion in his journey, he also had to find himself at the right place at the right time. And luckily, he did.

Joseph's story begins more than 33 years ago, when he was adopted at birth by Jeanne Eakins, a 47-year-old nurse from Richmond Hill, Ontario. His upbringing was unorthodox, to put it mildly.

When he was still a preschooler, his mother moved to nearby Gormley, where she married her second husband, Harold Joseph, and bought a special-care home for men

suffering from brain-related injuries. Hockey was not a priority.

The care home placed enormous demands on Joseph's parents. Often alone, Joseph and his older brother Grant retreated to the backyard, where they ran and jumped—and where Grant took shots on Curtis.

Still, Joseph never saw the ice.

Jeanne worried that Joseph, who was a rather small child, would be injured in ice hockey, so she allowed him only to play just outside the house. "There was a time," observes hockey writer Mike Ulmer, "when the anointed savior of the Leafs looked as though he'd never get past the family driveway."

And then fate smiled on Joseph—the first of several times. Joseph's sister, who was 22 years Curtis's senior, was moving, and had to pull her stepson out of a local hockey house-league.

It was too late for her to recover the enrollment fee, so she asked her mother if Curtis could take the spot. She explained that the equipment would keep him safe.

Joseph's mother said she'd let him dress for a tryout—but only that.

"They put him on the ice and they took shots at him for 15 minutes," recalls Joseph's sister Karen. "They couldn't get a puck past him, but they had to help him up because he couldn't stand properly in the skates. The coach came over and said: 'If this kid learns to skate, he's NHL material' "

Jeanne Eakins gave in, and Joseph joined the team—which was in last place when he came aboard. They finished the season in first.

The goalie was just getting going. Joseph, who's often been described as modest, generous, and a genuine nice guy, adored playing hockey, but dared not dream of the big leagues.

"I didn't think I was NHL caliber," he says. "I played Tier Two for two years and I should have been scouted, but the league wasn't that formidable. There were just four or five teams."

When Joseph was 17, his parents retired and moved to Nova Scotia, leaving their son to finish high school in Ontario. By the time he was 20, he'd reached his last year of junior eligibility, and prospects seemed remote.

Then, once again, something remarkable happened.

A man named Paul Sanders, who worked in a grocery store that the Eakin's had often patronized, decided to call up Notre Dame College in Wilcox, Saskatchewan. Sanders had long thought that Joseph had talent, and he knew Notre Dame was looking for talented players.

Joseph was instantly accepted.

"I honestly believe that if it wasn't for Notre Dame," says Sanders, "he would be installing swimming pools in Newmarket for $10 an hour."

The dream, at last, seemed achievable. Joseph was approached by two colleges after playing only two periods of his first exhibition game.

He went to the University of Wisconsin, where he ended up as runner-up for the Hobey Baker Award, given annually to the top college player in the U.S.

On June 16, 1989, he was signed as a free agent by the St. Louis Blues.

He remained there for six years, during which time he reached 100 wins in fewer games than any other Blues netminder. He finished among the leaders for the Vezina Trophy three times, and in one year recorded an amazing 36 wins.

He'd come a long way from the family driveway.

Still, the Blues didn't fare well in the play-offs during that time, and in August 1995, Joseph was traded to Edmonton. Two years

"I love my hockey. But if you can do that and go home and just be a dad and husband, then you have the best of both worlds."

later, as an unrestricted free agent, it was Joseph's turn to decide where he wanted to play. He opted for Toronto.

"Growing up just north of Toronto, I idolized most of the players who played on the Maple Leafs," says "Cujo", who was handed his nickname by Robert Dirk when they were teammates in St. Louis. "To actually put the sweater on and be part of the Maple Leafs is extremely exciting."

Exciting is also a word the folks in Toronto might use. Toronto did extremely well in Joseph's first season with the club, advancing to the Stanley Cup semifinals before being knocked out by Buffalo.

Now close to his roots again, Curtis lives on a 53-acre farm just north of Toronto with wife Nancy, their three children and their horses. Brother Grant, Joseph's original backyard teammate, lives nearby.

Still, when you meet Curtis Joseph, you get the feeling that success hasn't spoiled him a bit. In fact, you get the feeling he's just your average suburban dad.

"A reporter from Edmonton once called me asking for dirt on Curtis," says Joseph's boyhood pal Martin Harding. "I just laughed."

Curtis Joseph may have overcome the obstacles and arrived at a place that most kids only fantasize about, but the journey hasn't hurt him. If anything, it's helped him to see what matters most of all.

"I love my hockey," he says, "but if you can do that and go home and just be a dad and husband, then you have the best of both worlds."

Joseph is the kind of guy who thinks constantly of kids—and not just his own. Cujo has a kind of extended family that includes numerous sick children from across Canada who are routinely invited as his guests on hockey nights. "Cujo's Kids" watch the game from a private suite and are provided with food and autographs and invited into the Maple Leafs' dressing room following the game. "A lot of people ask me if one of my own kids has a medical problem, [that being] the reason I do this," says the father of three. "I tell them no, it's because I feel so lucky that my own family is healthy."

Year	Team	Lea	REGULAR SEASON								PLAYOFFS						
			GP	W	L	T	Mins	GA	SO	Avg	GP	W	L	Mins	GA	SO	Avg
1988-89	Univ. Wisconsin	WCHA	38	21	11	5	2267	94	1	2.49	....	....	....	....	....	....	....
1989-90	St. Louis	NHL	15	9	5	1	852	48	0	3.38	6	4	1	327	18	0	3.30
	Peoria Rivermen	IHL	23	10	8	2	1241	80	0	3.87	....	....	....	....	....	....	....
1990-91	St. Louis	NHL	30	16	10	2	1710	89	0	3.12	....	....	....	....	....	....	....
1991-92	St. Louis	NHL	60	27	20	10	3494	175	2	3.01	6	2	4	379	23	0	3.64
1992-93	St. Louis	NHL	68	29	28	9	3890	196	1	3.02	11	7	4	715	27	2	2.27
1993-94	St. Louis	NHL	71	36	23	11	4127	213	1	3.10	4	0	4	246	15	0	3.66
1994-95	St. Louis	NHL	36	20	10	1	1914	89	1	2.79	7	3	3	392	24	0	3.67
1995-96	Las Vegas	IHL	15	12	2	1	874	29	1	1.99	....	....	....	....	....	....	....
	Edmonton	NHL	34	15	16	2	1936	111	0	3.44	....	....	....	....	....	....	....
	Canada	WC-A	8	....	....	....	409	12	....	1.94	....	....	....	....	....	....	....
1996-97	Canada	W Cup	7	5	2	0	468	18	1	2.00	....	....	....	....	....	....	....
	Edmonton	NHL	72	32	29	9	4100	200	6	2.93	12	5	7	767	36	2	2.82
1997-98	Edmonton	NHL	71	29	31	9	4132	181	8	2.63	12	5	7	716	23	3	1.93
	Canada	Olympics	DID NOT PLAY - SPARE GOALTENDER														
1998-99	Toronto	NHL	67	35	24	7	4001	171	3	2.56	17	9	8	1011	41	1	2.43

Guy Hebert

31 ANAHEIM MIGHTY DUCKS

Six years ago, Guy Hebert little knew what fate was about to toss him. It was a warm June day, and the easygoing goaltender from upstate New York was off doing what he loved most: catching fish.

When he returned, his younger brother Jay passed on the news: Hebert would be heading clear across the country. He'd be tending the net for some expansion team that was owned by Disney, some team with a mighty funny name.

Hebert wasn't even sure where Anaheim was, only that it was somewhere south of Los Angeles. Still, he liked the notion of becoming a No. 1 goalie, of doing more than working back-up to Curtis Joseph in St. Louis.

He also liked the fact that the Mighty Ducks had plucked him first, before any other player. The job, he decided, would be a good one.

Hebert was absolutely right. Life in The Pond has turned out to be mighty good indeed.

Today, the 32-year-old Hebert has the distinction of being an original Mighty Duck. Teammates Paul Kariya and Teemu Selanne may have more national notoriety, and perhaps a lot more flash, but just one Mighty Duck has been with the club since Day One. Guy Hebert.

It has, quite literally, been the time of Hebert's life. He bought a house in Tustin, married his longtime sweetheart, and became father to a baby girl. And oh yes, he proved he was one heck of a goaltender.

Hebert was part of the United States team that won the World Cup hockey title in 1996, and a member of the American team that participated in the Nagano Olympics. It's what he's done in the NHL, however, that's truly endeared him to his fans.

"Guy is special," says Ducks general manager Pierre Gauthier. "He's an original Mighty Duck and means a lot to this franchise."

In 1998–99, Guy's play —in Selanne's assessment—was "unbelievable." He ended the season with a 31-29-9 record. He also managed his best-ever goals-against average, of 2.42, and a career-high 6 shutouts.

When Hebert plays his game, he's a master of the basics. He's not out to dazzle the crowd with flashy flops or dives—he simply wants to guard his net. He has, he says, been called "a pretty normal goalie."

"I think people underestimate how competitive he is," observes Ducks coach Craig Hartsburg. "When you talk to him, he's very laid-back and he's got a good sense of humor.

"But I've noticed, when he pulls that mask over him, there is a competitive edge that comes over him as well. In a game, he fights and battles and does everything he can to stop the puck."

> **When Hebert plays his game, he's a master of the basics. He's not out to dazzle the crowd with flashy flops or dives—he simply wants to guard his net.**

But hockey, of course, has been part of Hebert for an awfully long time. After all, his father didn't settle·on just any old name for his boy—he named him after the legendary Guy Lafleur of the Montreal Canadiens.

"I don't think my parents could have picked a better name for me," says Hebert. "I look back and think that my dad must have known something or had a hunch about what I'd be doing."

As a boy growing up in Troy, New York, Hebert's interest in hockey jockeyed with his passion for fly-fishing. He and his older brother would routinely head off on their bikes, fishing poles in hand, to try their luck at Cooper's Pond. As a kid he caught a sunfish; as an adult, it was a 120-pound tarpon, which he claims to have wrestled from a hammerhead shark while on a fishing trip to the Florida Keys.

As a young man, Hebert found himself picking up a hockey stick more frequently than a fishing rod. He played four years of NCAA hockey with Hamilton College, going 39-27-2, then joined the IHL in Peoria. In the 1987 NHL entry draft, he was picked up by the St. Louis Blues.

Today, however, Hebert seems completely rooted to his California home—and just as committed to his team.

"Looking back, my two years in Peoria in the IHL and my time with the St. Louis Blues seem like my college days, because it's so far away right now. It seems like I've been a Mighty Duck my entire career."

Indeed, Hebert would be perfectly content knowing The Pond was home ice for the rest of his hockey days.

"I really feel the team is going in the right direction and I'd hate to miss out on the good times after all the work I've put in to help the team get to this point," he says.

"I want to end my career here, and maybe have a Stanley Cup to go along with it."

As chief goalie for a team owned by the Disney empire, Guy Hebert has occasionally found himself in the spotlight—off the ice as well as on it. Hebert has done the voice-over for the Saturday morning "Mighty Ducks" cartoon show and appeared in an ESPN SportsCenter spot with figure skater Tai Babalonia. Recently, Hebert faced the cameras to tape an ESPN promotional feature at the Ducks' training facility. During that spot, Hebert talked about how luck had nothing to do with his success as a goalie. Just as he skated away from the crease, a 5,000-pound anvil dropped to the ice. "Very funny, guys," said Hebert as the cameras rolled.

Year	Team	Lea	REGULAR SEASON								PLAYOFFS						
			GP	W	L	T	Mins	GA	SO	Avg	GP	W	L	Mins	GA	SO	Avg
1985-86	Hamilton	NCAA	18	4	12	2	1011	69	2	4.09	....	....	....	....	....	....	....
1986-87	Hamilton	NCAA	18	12	5	0	1070	40	3	2.19	2	1	1	134	6	0	2.69
1987-88	Hamilton	NCAA	9	5	3	0	510	22	1	2.58	1	0	1	60	3	0	3.00
1988-89	Hamilton	NCAA	25	18	7	0	1454	62	2	2.56	2	1	1	126	4	0	1.90
1989-90	Peoria	IHL	30	7	13	7	1706	124	1	4.36	2	0	1	76	5	0	3.95
1990-91	Peoria	IHL	36	24	10	1	2093	100	2	2.87	8	3	4	458	32	0	4.19
1991-92	St. Louis	NHL	13	5	5	1	738	36	0	2.93	....	....	....	....	....	....	....
	Peoria	IHL	29	20	9	0	1731	98	0	3.40	4	3	1	239	9	0	2.26
1992-93	St. Louis	NHL	24	8	8	2	1210	74	1	3.67	1	0	0	2	0	0	0.00
1993-94	Anaheim	NHL	52	20	27	3	2991	141	2	2.83	....	....	....	....	....	....	....
	United States	WC-A	6	4	2	0	300	18	....	3.60	....	....	....	....	....	....	....
1994-95	Anaheim	NHL	39	12	20	4	2092	109	2	3.13	....	....	....	....	....	....	....
1995-96	Anaheim	NHL	59	28	23	5	3326	157	4	2.83	....	....	....	....	....	....	....
1996-97	United States	W Cup	1	....	....	....	60	3	0	3.00	....	....	....	....	....	....	....
	Anaheim	NHL	67	29	25	12	3863	172	4	2.67	9	4	4	534	18	1	2.02
1997-98	Anaheim	NHL	46	13	24	6	2660	130	3	2.93	....	....	....	....	....	....	....
1998-99	Anaheim	NHL	69	31	29	9	4083	165	6	2.42	4	0	3	208	15	0	4.33

Nikolai Khabibulin

35 PHOENIX COYOTES

As a young man growing up in Russia, Nikolai Khabibulin had a secret dream: to play a game in the National Hockey League.

After all, he'd long known that hockey was his passion. He also knew that goaltending was his position—he'd been firm about that ever since he'd watched his hero, the legendary Vladislav Tretiak. But he also believed that the NHL was the best league in the world, and that's where he longed to be.

The dream, of course, came true.

The outgoing kid from Sverdlovsk, the kid who's become known as Nik and Habby and The Bulin Wall, not only made it to the big leagues. He also made one heck of a big impression. Khabibulin, described by one sports writer as "the peasant-turned-prince-in-waiting," is currently ranked among the game's top goaltenders. In 1998–99, he played in 63 games for the Phoenix Coyotes, and finished with a save percentage of .923 and a goals-against average of 2.13. Back in January, that kind of play earned him a berth in the All-Star Game in Tampa, Florida where he joined Dominik Hasek as one of three European goalies representing the World team.

"A good goaltender gives you the

opportunity to win every hockey game," says former Coyotes coach Jim Schoenfeld. "Nik is like that."

Indeed he is. He is, as Coyotes GM Bobby Smith puts it, "an outstanding No. 1 goalie," a workhorse who played an astounding [both regular season and playoffs] 70 games with Phoenix last year, when backup Jimmy Waite was injured, and 72 the year before, the Coyotes' first in Phoenix after moving from Winnipeg.

It was back in 1992 that Habby was plucked by the Jets as their 8th choice—204th overall—in the NHL Entry Draft. He remained in Russia for a couple of years, playing on a Russian amateur team, and made his NHL debut in January 1995. He lost that game, but did well enough

during the season to be honored as the Jets' 1994–95 rookie of the year.

A year later, though, it was the league's turn to stand up and really take note. That, of course, was on April 26, 1996, when the Jets were facing playoff elimination, trailing Detroit three games to one. Khabibulin allowed just one goal among the 52 shots that were fired his way. The Jets won 3-1 that night, and Khabibulin pulled off what some consider one of the best playoff goaltending performances of the decade.

"I've played nine years and I've seen a lot of

"As a child, I watched Vladislav Tretiak, he was my hero, and because of him, I decided I wanted to play goalie."

games," said teammate Kris King at the time, "but I've never seen a guy win a game like that."

He wasn't the only one. Everyone at the game was astounded, seemingly even Khabibulin himself. "I think [it was my] best game ever," he said after his performance. "That's my most saves ever."

Khabibulin, who's 26, grew up in a middle-class family. The household revolved around sports: his father was a high-jumper and his mother, a runner. Khabibulin tried a bit of everything when he was young—soccer, tennis and handball—but his favorite sport, by far, was hockey. It took him a while, however, to decide which position he'd play.

Khabibulin never even tried playing goal until the age of 10, and then ended up gravitating toward defense. But then something—or rather, someone—inspired Khabibulin to

He comes out of the net to challenge all shooter —something Russian goaltenders are not taught to do—and he has a lightning-fast glove hand and a trademark acrobatic butterfly style.

strap on the goalie pads for good.

"As a child, I watched Vladislav Tretiak, he was my hero, and because of him, I decided I wanted to play goalie."

Hockey watchers say the six-foot-one, 195-pound Khabibulin does not conform to the Soviet stereotype, either on or off the ice. He likes to make his teammates laugh and is as laid-back and easygoing as anyone on the team. Khabibulin also tends toward a more North American style of netminding. He comes out of the net to challenge all shooters—something Russian goaltenders are not taught to do—and he has a lightning-fast glove hand

and a trademark acrobatic butterfly style.

Khabibulin has come a long way from the mining town where he was born, and along the way he's had to make multiple adjustments, not the least of which was learning a new language and adapting to a new culture.

And yes, he's also learned something else: that some dreams are truly worth pursuing.

Nikolai Khabibulin doesn't have to think too hard to come up with the fantasy Dream Team he'd want playing in front of him in Phoenix. First of all, he'd draft The Great (and recently-retired) Wayne Gretzky. Then he'd pull another pair of greats out of retirement: Mario Lemieux and Vladimir Fetisov. And for good measure, Khabibulin would include Ray Bourque and Jaromir Jagr. The only problem, admits the Phoenix netminder, is that he probably wouldn't see a lot of action. "I think most of the game would be played in the other zone," he says, "but I'd have the best seat in the house!"

Year	Team	Lea	GP	W	L	T	Mins	GA	SO	Avg	GP	W	L	Mins	GA	SO	Avg
							REGULAR SEASON							**PLAYOFFS**			
1988-89	Sverdlovsk	USSR	1	....	....	....	3	0	0	0.00	....	....	....	....	....	....	....
1989-90	Sverdlovsk,Jrs.	USSR					UNAVAILABLE										
1990-91	Sputnik	USSR 3					UNAVAILABLE										
1991-92	CSKA Moscow	CIS	2	....	....	....	34	2	0	3.52	....	....	....	....	....	....	....
1992-93	CSKA Moscow	CIS	13	....	....	....	491	27	0	3.29	....	....	....	....	....	....	....
1993-94	CSKA Moscow	CIS	46	....	....	....	2625	116	0	2.65	3	....	....	193	11	....	3.42
	Russian Pen's	IHL	12	2	7	2	639	47	0	4.41	....	....	....	....	....	....	....
1994-95	Springfield	AHL	23	9	9	3	1240	80	0	3.87	....	....	....	....	....	....	....
	Winnipeg	NHL	26	8	9	4	1339	76	0	3.41	....	....	....	....	....	....	....
1995-96	Winnipeg	NHL	53	26	20	3	2914	152	2	3.13	6	2	4	359	19	0	3.18
1996-97	Phoenix	NHL	72	30	33	6	4091	193	7	2.83	7	3	4	426	15	1	2.11
1997-98	Phoenix	NHL	70	30	28	10	4026	184	4	2.74	4	2	1	185	13	0	4.22
1998-99	Phoenix	NHL	63	32	23	7	3657	130	8	2.13	7	3	4	449	18	0	2.41

Vezina Trophy Winners

1999 Dominik Hasek, Buffalo Sabres	**1966** Gump Worsley, Montreal Canadians
1998 Dominik Hasek, Buffalo Sabres	Charlie Hodge, Montreal Canadians
1997 Dominik Hasek, Buffalo Sabres	**1965** Terry Sawchuk, Toronto Maple Leafs
1996 Jim Carey, Washington Capitals	Johnny Bower, Toronto Maple Leafs
1995 Dominik Hasek, Buffalo Sabres	**1964** Charlie Hodge, Montreal Canadiens
1994 Dominik Hasek, Buffalo Sabres	**1963** Glenn Hall, Chicago Blackhawks
1993 Ed Belfour, Chicago Blackhawks	**1962** Jacques Plante, Montreal Canadiens
1992 Patrick Roy, Montreal Canadiens	**1961** Johnny Bower, Toronto Maple Leafs
1991 Ed Belfour, Chicago Blackhawks	**1960** Jacques Plante, Montreal Canadiens
1990 Patrick Roy, Montreal Canadiens	**1959** Jacques Plante, Montreal Canadiens
1989 Patrick Roy, Montreal Canadiens	**1958** Jacques Plante, Montreal Canadiens
1988 Grant Fuhr, Edmonton Oilers	**1957** Jacques Plante, Montreal Canadiens
1987 Ron Hextall, Philadelphia Flyers	**1956** Jacques Plante, Montreal Canadiens
1986 John Vanbiesbrouck, New York Rangers	**1955** Terry Sawchuk, Detroit Red Wings
1985 Pelle Lindbergh, Philadelphia Flyers	**1954** Harry Lumley, Toronto Maple Leafs
1984 Tom Barrasso, Buffalo Sabres	**1953** Terry Sawchuk, Detroit Red Wings
1983 Pete Peeters, Boston Bruins	**1952** Terry Sawchuk, Detroit Red Wings
1982 Billy Smith, New York Islanders	**1951** Al Rollins, Toronto Maple Leafs
1981 Richard Sevigny, Montreal Canadiens	**1950** Bill Durnan, Montreal Canadiens
Denis Herron, Montreal Canadiens	**1949** Bill Durnan, Montreal Canadiens
Michel Larocque, Montreal Canadiens	**1948** Turk Broda, Toronto Maple Leafs
1980 Bob Sauve, Buffalo Sabres	**1947** Bill Durnan, Montreal Canadiens
Don Edwards, Buffalo Sabres	**1946** Bill Durnan, Montreal Canadiens
1979 Ken Dryden, Montreal Canadiens	**1945** Bill Durnan, Montreal Canadiens
Michel Larocque, Montreal Canadiens	**1944** Bill Durnan, Montreal Canadiens
1978 Ken Dryden, Montreal Canadiens	**1943** Johnny Mowers, Detroit Red Wings
Michel Larocque, Montreal Canadiens	**1942** Frank Brimsek, Boston Bruins
1977 Ken Dryden, Montreal Canadiens	**1941** Turk Broda, Toronto Maple Leafs
Michel Larocque, Montreal Canadiens	**1940** Dave Kerr, New York Rangers
1976 Ken Dryden, Montreal Canadiens	**1939** Frank Brimsek, Boston Bruins
1975 Bernie Parent, Philadelphia Flyers	**1938** Tiny Thompson, Boston Bruins
1974 Bernie Parent, Philadelphia Flyers (tie)	**1937** Normie Smith, Detroit Red Wings
Tony Esposito, Chicago Blackhawks (tie)	**1936** Tiny Thompson, Boston Bruins
1973 Ken Dryden, Montreal Canadiens	**1935** Lorne Chabot, Chicago Blackhawks
1972 Tony Esposito, Chicago Blackhawks	**1934** Charlie Gardiner, Chicago Blackhawks
Gary Smith, Chicago Blackhawks	**1933** Tiny Thompson, Boston Bruins
1971 Ed Giacomin, New York Rangers	**1932** Charlie Gardiner, Chicago Blackhawks
Gilles Villemure, New York Rangers	**1931** Roy Worters, New York Americans
1970 Tony Esposito, Chicago Blackhawks	**1930** Tiny Thompson, Boston Bruins
1969 Jacques Plante, St. Louis Blues	**1929** George Hainsworth, Montreal Canadiens
Glenn Hall, St. Louis Blues	**1928** George Hainsworth, Montreal Canadiens
1968 Gump Worsley, Montreal Canadiens	**1927** George Hainsworth, Montreal Canadiens
Rogatien Vachon, Montreal Canadiens	
1967 Glenn Hall, Chicago Blackhawks	
Denis DeJordy, Chicago Blackhawks	

Photo Credits

Alison Mooney: p.104-Hockey Equipment Illustrations

David Bier/HHOF: p.5-Jacques Plante

Doug MacLellan/HHOF: p.74-Plante Mask, p.75-1972 mask, p.76-1980 mask, p.100-skates

Frank Prazak/HHOF: p.2-Tony Esposito, p.30-Eddie Giacomin, p.33-Johnny Bower, p.43-Ken Dryden

Graphic Artists/HHOF: p.3-Terry Sawchuk/Johnny Bower, p.7-Glenn Hall, p.128-Ken Dryden

HHOF: p.8-Turk Broda/Bill Durnan, p.36-George Vezina, p.75-1961 mask, p.76-1990 Mask, p.77-Gerry Cheevers

Imperial Oil-Turofsky/HHOF: p.32-Gump Worsley, p.34-Turk Broda, p.35-Terry Sawchuck

London Life-Portnoy/HHOF: p.126-Glen Hanlon

NHL Images: p.152-Vezina Trophy

NHL Images/Andrew Bernstein: p.51-Chris Osgood, p.57-Mike Dunham, p.66-Chris Osgood, p.81-Patrick Roy

NHL Images/Barry Gossage: p.37-Trevor Kidd, p.151-Nikolai Khabibulin

NHL Images/Brian Babineau: p.19-Ron Tugnutt

NHL Images/Craig Melvin: p.9-Chris Osgood/Patrick Roy, p.11-Dominik Hasek, p.21-Ron Tugnutt, p.22-Ron Tugnutt, p.87-Mike Richter, p.129-Patrick Roy, p.141-Guy Hebert, p.143-Guy Hebert, p.144-Guy Hebert, p.150-Nikolai Khabibulin

NHL Images/Diane Sobolewski: p.119-Byron Dafoe

NHL Images/Dave Sandford: p.vi-Stephan Fiset, p.6-John Vanbiesbrouck, p.10-Dominik Hasek, p.12-Dominik Hasek, p.15-Dominik Hasek, p.16-Dominik Hasek, p.18-Ron Tugnutt, p.20-Ron Tugnutt, p.25-Olag Kolzig, p.26-Olaf Kolzig, p.28-Olaf Kolzig, p.40-Curtis Joseph, p.41-Mike Vernon, p.46-Ed Belfour, p.47-Ed Belfour p.52-Chris Osgood, p.56-Mike Dunham, p.61-Ron Tugnutt, p.68-Byron Dafoe, p.72-Jamie Storr, p.78-Ed Belfour, p.78-Curtis Joseph, p.82-Patrick Roy, p.84-Patrick Roy, p.86-Mike Richter, p.88-Mike Richter, p.90-Mike Richter, p.98-Mike Richter, p.108-Martin Brodeur, p.109-Martin Brodeur, p.110-Martin Brodeur, p.112-Martin Brodeur, p.114-Byron Dafoe, p.116-Byron Dafoe, p.117-Byron Dafoe, p.118-Byron Dafoe, p.120-John Vanbiesbrouck, p.121-John Vanbiesbrouck, p.123-John Vanbiesbrouck, p.132-Martin Brodeur, p.133-Dominik

Hasek, p.134-Curtis Joseph, p.135-Curtis Joseph, p.136-Curtis Joseph, p.137-Curtis Joseph, p.138-Curtis Joseph, p.146-Nikolai Khabibulin, p.149-Nikolai Khabibulin

NHL Images/Tim DeFrisco: p.ii-Brathwaite, p.92-Steve Shields, p.122-John Vanbiesbrouck

NHL Images/Don Smith: p.48-Ed Belfour, p.93-Steve Shields, p.95-Steve Shields, p.96-Steve Shields

NHL Images/AB/Garrett Ellwood: p.38-Jamie Storr, p.60-Mike Dunham

NHL Images/Glenn James: p.140-Guy Hebert

NHL Images/Mitchell Layton: p.27-Olaf Kolzig, p.54-Chris Osgood, p.64-Olag Kolzig, p.89-Mike Richter, p.106-John Vanbiesbrouck, p.124-John Vanbiesbrouck

NHL Images/Nat Butler: p.79-Mike Richter

NHL Images/Nevin Reid: p.4-Patrick Roy, p.24-Olaf Kolzig, p.80-Patrick Roy

NHL Images/Paul Bereswell: p.50-Chris Osgood, p.53-Chris Osgood

NHL Images/Ray Garbowski: p.94-Steve Shields, p.44-Ed Belfour, p.45-Ed Belfour, p.70-John Vanbiesbrouck, p.147-Nikolai Khabibulin

NHL Images/AB/Robert Mora: p.131-Darren Puppa

NHL Images/Ron Vesely: p.58-Mike Dunham, p.59-Mike Dunham, p.142-Guy Hebert

NHL Images/Steve Babineau: p.115-Byron Dafoe, p.145-Guy Hebert, p.148-Nikolai Khabibulin

---

Acknowledgments

Many of the quotes contained in this book first appeared in newspapers, magazines, books and in-house publications of NHL teams throughout the United States and Canada. The authors would like to acknowledge:

The Philadelphia Daily News
The Delaware County Times
The Philadelphia Inquirer
The Ottawa Sun
The Ottawa Citizen
The Orange County Register
The Pasadena Star News
Harnett's Sports Arizona
The Boston Herald
The Boston Globe
Face-off: In the Crease
San Jose Sharks Magazine
The Sporting News
Hockey Illustrated
The Tennessean
The New York Post
The New York Daily News
Newsday
The Detroit Free Press
The Toronto Sun
The Toronto Star
Saturday Night
Hockey Night in Toronto
Men's Journal
The Vancouver Sun
The New York Times
Newark Star-Ledger
Continental Magazine
ESPN Magazine
Rocky Mountain News
Denver Post
The Buffalo News
USA Today
The Washington Post

In the Crease: Goaltenders Look at Life in the NHL. By Dick Irwin (McClelland and Stewart, 1995)

The Official NHL 75th Anniversary Commemorative Book, Dan Diamond, Ed. (Firefly Books, 1991)

Hockey Hall of Fame: The Official Registry of the Games Honour Roll, Dan Diamond, Ed. (Doubleday, 1996)

The Game, By Ken Dryden. (Macmillan of Canada, 1983)

The Art of Goaltending, By Vladislav Tretiak. (Plaine Publishing, 1989)

Also: The Media Relations Department of the National Hockey League teams whose goaltenders are profiled in this book.